# Contents

Yamaha DT50 MX 1983 model

# Yamaha DT 50 & 80 Trail Bikes Owners Workshop Manual

## by Chris Rogers

**Models covered**
DT50 M. 49.9cc. Introduced January 1978, discontinued July 1982
DT50 MX. 49.9cc. Introduced June 1981
DT80 MX. 79.0cc. Introduced April 1981

**ISBN 0 85696 800 5**

Printed in England

THE BOOK

**HAYNES PUBLISHING GROUP**
**SPARKFORD YEOVIL SOMERSET BA22 7JJ ENGLAND**
*distributed in the USA by*
**HAYNES PUBLICATIONS INC**
**861 LAWRENCE DRIVE**
**NEWBURY PARK**
**CALIFORNIA 91320**
**USA**

# Acknowledgements

Special thanks are due to Jim Patch of Yeovil Motor Cycle Services for his help in supplying technical information and for the DT50 MX model featured throughout this Manual.

Mitsui Machinery Sales (UK) Limited gave permission to use the line drawings contained in this Manual and supplied much of the technical information used by the Author.

Thanks are also due to the Avon Rubber Company, who kindly supplied information and technical assistance on tyre fitting; NGK Spark Plugs (UK) Ltd for information on spark plug maintenance and electrode conditions, and Renold Ltd for advice on chain care and renewal.

# About this manual

The purpose of this manual is to present the owner with a concise and graphic guide which will enable him to tackle any operation from basic routine maintenance to a major overhaul. It has been assumed that any work would be undertaken without the luxury of a well-equipped workshop and a range of manufacturer's service tools.

To this end, the machine featured in the manual was stripped and rebuilt in our own workshop, by a team comprising a mechanic, a photographer and the author. The resulting photographic sequence depicts events as they took place, the hands shown being those of the author and the mechanic.

The use of specialised, and expensive, service tools was avoided unless their use was considered to be essential due to risk of breakage or injury. There is usually some way of improvising a method of removing a stubborn component, providing that a suitable degree of care is exercised.

The author learnt his motorcycle mechanics over a number of years, faced with the same difficulties and using similar facilities to those encountered by most owners. It is hoped that this practical experience can be passed on through the pages of this manual.

Where possible, a well-used example of the machine is chosen for the workshop project, as this highlights any areas which might be particularly prone to giving rise to problems. In this way, any such difficulties are encountered and resolved before the text is written, and the techniques used to deal with them can be incorporated in the relevant section. Armed with a working knowledge of the machine, the author undertakes a considerable amount of research in order that the maximum amount of data can be included in the manual.

A comprehensive section, preceding the main part of the manual, describes procedures for carrying out the routine maintenance of the machine at intervals of time and mileage. This section is included particularly for those owners who wish to ensure the efficient day-to-day running of their motorcycle, but who choose not to undertake overhaul or renovation work.

Each Chapter is divided into numbered sections. Within these sections are numbered paragraphs. Cross reference throughout the manual is quite straightforward and logical. When reference is made 'See Section 6.10' it means Section 6, paragraph 10 in the same Chapter. If another Chapter were intended, the reference would read, for example, 'See Chapter 2, Section 6.10'. All the photographs are captioned with a section/paragraph number to which they refer and are relevant to the Chapter text adjacent.

Figures (usually line illustrations) appear in a logical but numerical order, within a given Chapter. Fig. 1.1 therefore refers to the first figure in Chapter 1.

Left-hand and right-hand descriptions of the machines and their components refer to the left and right of a given machine when the rider is seated normally.

Motorcycle manufacturers continually make changes to specifications and recommendations, and these, when notified, are incorporated into our manuals at the earliest opportunity.

Whilst every care is taken to ensure that the information in this manual is correct no liability can be accepted by the author or publishers for loss, damage or injury caused by any errors in or omissions from the information given.

Close-up of engine of Yamaha DT50 MX

# Introduction to the Yamaha DT50 and 80 models

Although the history of Yamaha can be traced back to the year 1887, when a then very small company commenced manufacture of reed organs, it was not until 1954 that the company became interested in motorcycles. As can be imagined, the problems of marketing a motorcycle against a background of musical instruments manufacture were considerable. Some local racing successes helped achieve the desired results and in July 1955 the Yamaha Motor Company was established as a separate entity, employing a work force of less than 100 and turning out some 300 machines a month.

Competition successes continued and Yamaha became established as one of the world's leading motorcycle manufacturers. Part of this success story is the impressive list of Yamaha 'firsts' — a whole string of innovations that includes electric starting, pressed steel frame, torque induction, 6- and 8-port engines and the Autolube system of lubrication.

Turning their attention to the market being formed around the rapidly growing number of riders who wished to spend their leisure hours riding both on and off the road, Yamaha introduced a range of dual purpose machines covering the 50 cc to 400 cc capacity classes and carrying the DT prefix.

In January of 1978 the DT50 M was introduced to cater for the beginners' end of the market. The advances gained in frame and engine design through competition soon led to the DT50 M being superseded by the DT50 MX model. This machine, introduced in June of 1981, incorporated yet another Yamaha first, the monocross rear suspension system. A similar machine, the DT80 MX, followed soon afterwards in January of 1982.

# Model dimensions and weights

| | DT50 M | DT50 MX and 80 MX |
|---|---|---|
| Overall length | 1860 mm (73.2 in) | 2055 mm (80.9 in) |
| Overall width | 805 mm (31.7 in) | 835 mm (32.9 in) |
| Overall height | 1045 mm (41.1 in) | 1135 mm (44.7 in) |
| Wheelbase | 1210 mm (47.6 in) | 1280 mm (50.4 in) |
| Ground clearance | 225 mm (8.9 in) | 260 mm (10.2 in) |
| Seat height | 780 mm (30.7 in) | 820 mm (32.3 in) |
| Weight | 72 kg (159 lb) | 81 kg (180 lb) |

# Ordering spare parts

When ordering spare parts for any Yamaha, deal direct with an official Yamaha agent who should be able to supply most of the parts ex-stock. Parts cannot be obtained from Yamaha direct, even if the parts required are not held in stock. Always quote the engine and frame numbers in full, especially if parts are required for earlier models. The frame number is stamped on the steering head and the engine number on the left-hand crankcase half top surface.

Use only genuine Yamaha spares. Some pattern parts are available that are made in Japan and may be packed in similar looking packages. They should only be used if genuine parts are hard to obtain or in an emergency, for they do not normally last as long as genuine parts, even although there may be a price advantage.

Some of the more expendable parts such as spark plugs, bulbs, oils and greases etc, can be obtained from accessory shops and motor factors, who have convenient opening hours, and can be found not far from home. It is also possible to obtain parts on a Mail Order basis from a number of specialists who advertise regularly in the motorcycle magazines.

Location of frame number

Location of engine number

# Safety First!

Professional motor mechanics are trained in safe working procedures. However enthusiastic you may be about getting on with the job in hand, do take the time to ensure that your safety is not put at risk. A moment's lack of attention can result in an accident, as can failure to observe certain elementary precautions.

There will always be new ways of having accidents, and the following points do not pretend to be a comprehensive list of all dangers; they are intended rather to make you aware of the risks and to encourage a safety-conscious approach to all work you carry out on your vehicle.

## Essential DOs and DON'Ts

**DON'T** start the engine without first ascertaining that the transmission is in neutral.

**DON'T** suddenly remove the filler cap from a hot cooling system — cover it with a cloth and release the pressure gradually first, or you may get scalded by escaping coolant.

**DON'T** attempt to drain oil until you are sure it has cooled sufficiently to avoid scalding you.

**DON'T** grasp any part of the engine, exhaust or silencer without first ascertaining that it is sufficiently cool to avoid burning you.

**DON'T** syphon toxic liquids such as fuel, brake fluid or antifreeze by mouth, or allow them to remain on your skin.

**DON'T** inhale brake lining dust — it is injurious to health.

**DON'T** allow any spilt oil or grease to remain on the floor — wipe it up straight away, before someone slips on it.

**DON'T** use ill-fitting spanners or other tools which may slip and cause injury.

**DON'T** attempt to lift a heavy component which may be beyond your capability — get assistance.

**DON'T** rush to finish a job, or take unverified short cuts.

**DON'T** allow children or animals in or around an unattended vehicle.

**DON'T** inflate a tyre to a pressure above the recommended maximum. Apart from overstressing the carcase and wheel rim, in extreme cases the tyre may blow off forcibly.

**DO** ensure that the machine is supported securely at all times. This is especially important when the machine is blocked up to aid wheel or fork removal.

**DO** take care when attempting to slacken a stubborn nut or bolt. It is generally better to pull on a spanner, rather than push, so that if slippage occurs you fall away from the machine rather than on to it.

**DO** wear eye protection when using power tools such as drill, sander, bench grinder etc.

**DO** use a barrier cream on your hands prior to undertaking dirty jobs — it will protect your skin from infection as well as making the dirt easier to remove afterwards; but make sure your hands aren't left slippery.

**DO** keep loose clothing (cuffs, tie etc) and long hair well out of the way of moving mechanical parts.

**DO** remove rings, wristwatch etc, before working on the vehicle — especially the electrical system.

**DO** keep your work area tidy — it is only too easy to fall over articles left lying around.

**DO** exercise caution when compressing springs for removal or installation. Ensure that the tension is applied and released in a controlled manner, using suitable tools which preclude the possibility of the spring escaping violently.

**DO** ensure that any lifting tackle used has a safe working load rating adequate for the job.

**DO** get someone to check periodically that all is well, when working alone on the vehicle.

**DO** carry out work in a logical sequence and check that everything is correctly assembled and tightened afterwards.

**DO** remember that your vehicle's safety affects that of yourself and others. If in doubt on any point, get specialist advice.

**IF,** in spite of following these precautions, you are unfortunate enough to injure yourself, seek medical attention as soon as possible.

## Fire

Remember at all times that petrol (gasoline) is highly flammable. Never smoke, or have any kind of naked flame around, when working on the vehicle. But the risk does not end there — a spark caused by an electrical short-circuit, by two metal surfaces contacting each other, or even by static electricity built up in your body under certain conditions, can ignite petrol vapour, which in a confined space is highly explosive.

Always disconnect the battery earth (ground) terminal before working on any part of the fuel system, and never risk spilling fuel on to a hot engine or exhaust.

It is recommended that a fire extinguisher of a type suitable for fuel and electrical fires is kept handy in the garage or workplace at all times. Never try to extinguish a fuel or electrical fire with water.

## Fumes

Certain fumes are highly toxic and can quickly cause unconsciousness and even death if inhaled to any extent. Petrol (gasoline) vapour comes into this category, as do the vapours from certain solvents such as trichloroethylene. Any draining or pouring of such volatile fluids should be done in a well ventilated area.

When using cleaning fluids and solvents, read the instructions carefully. Never use materials from unmarked containers — they may give off poisonous vapours.

Never run the engine of a motor vehicle in an enclosed space such as a garage. Exhaust fumes contain carbon monoxide which is extremely poisonous; if you need to run the engine, always do so in the open air or at least have the rear of the vehicle outside the workplace.

If you are fortunate enough to have the use of an inspection pit, never drain or pour petrol, and never run the engine, while the vehicle is standing over it; the fumes, being heavier than air, will concentrate in the pit with possibly lethal results.

## The battery

Never cause a spark, or allow a naked light, near the vehicle's battery. It will normally be giving off a certain amount of hydrogen gas, which is highly explosive.

Always disconnect the battery earth (ground) terminal before working on the fuel or electrical systems.

If possible, loosen the filler plugs or cover when charging the battery from an external source. Do not charge at an excessive rate or the battery may burst.

Take care when topping up and when carrying the battery. The acid electrolyte, even when diluted, is very corrosive and should not be allowed to contact the eyes or skin.

If you ever need to prepare electrolyte yourself, always add the acid slowly to the water, and never the other way round. Protect against splashes by wearing rubber gloves and goggles.

## Mains electricity

When using an electric power tool, inspection light etc which works from the mains, always ensure that the appliance is correctly connected to its plug and that, where necessary, it is properly earthed (grounded). Do not use such appliances in damp conditions and, again, beware of creating a spark or applying excessive heat in the vicinity of fuel or fuel vapour.

## Ignition HT voltage

A severe electric shock can result from touching certain parts of the ignition system, such as the HT leads, when the engine is running or being cranked, particularly if components are damp or the insulation is defective. Where an electronic ignition system is fitted, the HT voltage is much higher and could prove fatal.

# Tools and working facilities

The first priority when undertaking maintenance or repair work of any sort on a motorcycle is to have a clean, dry, well-lit working area. Work carried out in peace and quiet in the well-ordered atmosphere of a good workshop will give more satisfaction and much better results than can usually be achieved in poor working conditions. A good workshop must have a clean flat workbench or a solidly constructed table of convenient working height. The workbench or table should be equipped with a vice which has a jaw opening of at least 4 in (100 mm). A set of jaw covers should be made from soft metal such as aluminium alloy or copper, or from wood. These covers will minimise the marking or damaging of soft or delicate components which may be clamped in the vice. Some clean, dry, storage space will be required for tools, lubricants and dismantled components. It will be necessary during a major overhaul to lay out engine/gearbox components for examination and to keep them where they will remain undisturbed for as long as is necessary. To this end it is recommended that a supply of metal or plastic containers of suitable size is collected. A supply of clean, lint-free, rags for cleaning purposes and some newspapers, other rags, or paper towels for mopping up spillages should also be kept. If working on a hard concrete floor note that both the floor and one's knees can be protected from oil spillages and wear by cutting open a large cardboard box and spreading it flat on the floor under the machine or workbench. This also helps to provide some warmth in winter and to prevent the loss of nuts, washers, and other tiny components which have a tendency to disappear when dropped on anything other than a perfectly clean, flat, surface.

Unfortunately, such working conditions are not always available to the home mechanic. When working in poor conditions it is essential to take extra time and care to ensure that the components being worked on are kept scrupulously clean and to ensure that no components or tools are lost or damaged.

A selection of good tools is a fundamental requirement for anyone contemplating the maintenance and repair of a motor vehicle. For the owner who does not possess any, their purchase will prove a considerable expense, offsetting some of the savings made by doing-it-yourself. However, provided that the tools purchased are of good quality, they will last for many years and prove an extremely worthwhile investment.

To help the average owner to decide which tools are needed to carry out the various tasks detailed in this manual, we have compiled three lists of tools under the following headings: *Maintenance and minor repair, Repair and overhaul,* and *Specialized.* The newcomer to practical mechanics should start off with the simpler jobs around the vehicle. Then, as his confidence and experience grow, he can undertake more difficult tasks, buying extra tools as and when they are needed. In this way, a *Maintenance and minor repair* tool kit can be built-up into a *Repair and overhaul* tool kit over a considerable period of time without any major cash outlays. The experienced home mechanic will have a tool kit good enough for most repair and overhaul procedures and will add tools from the specialized category when he feels the expense is justified by the amount of use these tools will be put to.

It is obviously not possible to cover the subject of tools fully here. For those who wish to learn more about tools and their use there is a book entitled *How to Choose and Use Car Tools* available from the publishers of this manual. Although, as its title implies, this publication is directed at car owners, the information given is equally applicable to motorcycle owners. It also provides an introduction to basic workshop practice which will be of interest to a home mechanic working on any type of motor vehicle.

As a general rule, it is better to buy the more expensive, good quality tools. Given reasonable use, such tools will last for a very long time, whereas the cheaper, poor quality, item will wear out faster and need to be renewed more often, thus nullifying the original saving. There is also the risk of a poor quality tool breaking while in use, causing personal injury or expensive damage to the component being worked on. It should be noted, however, that many car accessory shops and the large department stores sell tools of reasonable quality at competitive prices. The best example of this is found with socket sets, where a medium-priced socket set will be quite adequate for the home owner and yet prove less expensive than a selection of individual sockets and accessories. This is because individual pieces are usually only available from expensive, top quality, ranges and whilst they are undeniably good, it should be remembered that they are intended for professional use.

The basis of any toolkit is a set of spanners. While open-ended spanners with their slim jaws, are useful for working on awkwardly-positioned nuts, ring spanners have advantages in that they grip the nut far more positively. There is less risk of the spanner slipping off the nut and damaging it, for this reason alone ring spanners are to be preferred. Ideally, the home mechanic should acquire a set of each, but if expense rules this out a set of combination spanners (open-ended at one end and with a ring of the same size at the other) will provide a good compromise. Another item which is so useful it should be considered an essential requirement for any home mechanic is a set of socket spanners. These are available in a variety of drive sizes. It is recommended that the ½-inch drive type is purchased to begin with as although bulkier and more expensive than the ⅜-inch type, the larger size is far more common and will accept a greater variety of torque wrenches, extension pieces and socket sizes. The socket set should comprise sockets of sizes between 8 and 24 mm, a reversible ratchet drive, an extension bar of about 10 inches in length, a spark plug socket with a rubber insert, and a universal joint. Other attachments can be added to the set at a later date.

## Maintenance and minor repair tool kit

Set of spanners 8 – 24 mm
Set of sockets and attachments
Spark plug spanner with rubber insert – 10, 12, or 14 mm as appropriate
Adjustable spanner
C-spanner/pin spanner
Torque wrench (same size drive as sockets)
Set of screwdrivers (flat blade)
Set of screwdrivers (cross-head)
Set of Allen keys 4 – 10 mm
Impact screwdriver and bits
Ball pein hammer – 2 lb
Hacksaw (junior)
Self-locking pliers – Mole grips or vice grips
Pliers – combination
Pliers – needle nose
Wire brush (small)
Soft-bristled brush
Tyre pump
Tyre pressure gauge
Tyre tread depth gauge
Oil can
Fine emery cloth
Funnel (medium size)
Drip tray
Grease gun
Set of feeler gauges
Brake bleeding kit
Strobe timing light
Continuity tester (dry battery and bulb)
Soldering iron and solder
Wire stripper or craft knife
PVC insulating tape
Assortment of split pins, nuts, bolts, and washers

## Repair and overhaul toolkit

The tools in this list are virtually essential for anyone undertaking major repairs to a motorcycle and are additional to the tools listed above. Concerning Torx driver bits, Torx screws are encountered on some of the more modern machines where their use is restricted to fastening certain components inside the engine/gearbox unit. It is therefore recommended that if Torx bits cannot be borrowed from a local dealer, they are purchased individually as the need arises. They are not in regular use in the motor trade and will therefore only be available in specialist tool shops.

Plastic or rubber soft-faced mallet
Torx driver bits
Pliers – electrician's side cutters
Circlip pliers – internal (straight or right-angled tips are available)
Circlip pliers – external
Cold chisel
Centre punch
Pin punch
Scriber
Scraper (made from soft metal such as aluminium or copper)
Soft metal drift
Steel rule/straight edge
Assortment of files
Electric drill and bits

Wire brush (large)
Soft wire brush (similar to those used for cleaning suede shoes)
Sheet of plate glass
Hacksaw (large)
Valve grinding tool
Valve grinding compound (coarse and fine)
Stud extractor set (E-Z out)

## Specialized tools

This is not a list of the tools made by the machine's manufacturer to carry out a specific task on a limited range of models. Occasional references are made to such tools in the text of this manual and, in general, an alternative method of carrying out the task without the manufacturer's tool is given where possible. The tools mentioned in this list are those which are not used regularly and are expensive to buy in view of their infrequent use. Where this is the case it may be possible to hire or borrow the tools against a deposit from a local dealer or tool hire shop. An alternative is for a group of friends or a motorcycle club to join in the purchase.

Valve spring compressor
Piston ring compressor
Universal bearing puller
Cylinder bore honing attachment (for electric drill)
Micrometer set
Vernier calipers
Dial gauge set
Cylinder compression gauge
Vacuum gauge set
Multimeter
Dwell meter/tachometer

## Care and maintenance of tools

Whatever the quality of the tools purchased, they will last much longer if cared for. This means in practice ensuring that a tool is used for its intended purpose; for example screwdrivers should not be used as a substitute for a centre punch, or as chisels. Always remove dirt or grease and any metal particles but remember that a light film of oil will prevent rusting if the tools are infrequently used. The common tools can be kept together in a large box or tray but the more delicate, and more expensive, items should be stored separately where they cannot be damaged. When a tool is damaged or worn out, be sure to renew it immediately. It is false economy to continue to use a worn spanner or screwdriver which may slip and cause expensive damage to the component being worked on.

## Fastening systems

Fasteners, basically, are nuts, bolts and screws used to hold two or more parts together. There are a few things to keep in mind when working with fasteners. Almost all of them use a locking device of some type; either a lock washer, lock nut, locking tab or thread adhesive. All threaded fasteners should be clean, straight, have undamaged threads and undamaged corners on the hexagon head where the spanner fits. Develop the habit of replacing all damaged nuts and bolts with new ones.

Rusted nuts and bolts should be treated with a rust penetrating fluid to ease removal and prevent breakage. After applying the rust penetrant, let it 'work' for a few minutes before trying to loosen the nut or bolt. Badly rusted fasteners may have to be chiseled off or removed with a special nut breaker, available at tool shops.

Flat washers and lock washers, when removed from an assembly should always be replaced exactly as removed. Replace any damaged washers with new ones. Always use a flat washer between a lock washer and any soft metal surface (such as aluminium), thin sheet metal or plastic. Special lock nuts can only be used once or twice before they lose their locking ability and must be renewed.

If a bolt or stud breaks off in an assembly, it can be drilled out and removed with a special tool called an E-Z out. Most dealer service departments and motorcycle repair shops can perform this task, as well as others (such as the repair of threaded holes that have been stripped out).

# YAMAHA DT 50 & 80 TRAIL BIKES

## Recommended lubricants

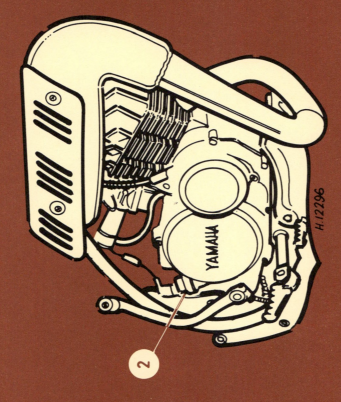

H.12296

| Component | | Quantity | Type/viscosity |
|---|---|---|---|
| **1** Engine | | 1.0 lit (1.76 Imp pt) | Good quality non-diluent 2-stroke oil SAE 10W/30 |
| **2** Gearbox – at oil change | | | SAE 10W/30 |
| | DT50 M | 550 cc (0.97 Imp pt) | |
| | All others | 600 cc (1.05 Imp pt) | |
| **3** Front forks | | | |
| | DT50 M | 140 cc (4.93 Imp fl oz) | SAE 10W/30 motor oil |
| | All others | 208 cc (7.32 Imp fl oz) | SAE 10 fork oil |
| **4** Final drive chain | | As required | Aerosol chain lubricant |
| **5** Wheel bearings | | As required | High melting point grease |
| **6** Steering head | | As required | High melting point |

## Adjustment data

| Tyre pressures | Front | Rear |
|---|---|---|
| DT50 M | 14 psi (1.0 kg/cm²) | 17 psi (1.2 kg/cm²) |
| All others | 21 psi (1.5 kg/cm²) | 26 psi (1.8 kg/cm²) |

| Spark plug type | |
|---|---|
| DT80 MX | NGK B8HS |
| All others | NGK B7HS |

**Spark plug gap**   0.6 mm (0.024 in)

**Contact breaker gap**   0.3 – 0.4 mm (0.011 – 0.015 in)

**Ignition timing**   1.65 – 1.95 mm (0.064 – 0.076 in) BTDC

| Idle speed | |
|---|---|
| DT50 MX | 1250 rpm |
| All others | 1300 rpm |

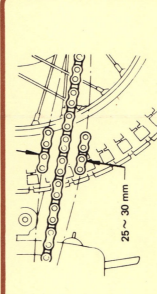

25 ~ 30 mm

Chain free play measurement

## Check list

### Daily

1   Check the level of engine oil in the tank

### Weekly or every 150 miles (250 km)

1   Check the machine for loose fittings and leaks
2   Check the operation of the lights, horn and speedometer
3   Check the tyre pressures
4   Inspect the tyres for wear and damage
5   Lubricate the exposed portions of control cables
6   Lubricate the final drive chain
7   Check the gearbox oil level

### Fortnightly or every 300 miles (500 km)

1   Adjust the final drive chain
2   Check the battery

### Monthly, or every 900 miles (1500 km)

1   Check the final drive chain for wear
2   Clean and examine the air filter

### Two monthly or every 1800 miles (3000 km)

1   Change the gearbox oil
2   Adjust the clutch
3   Adjust the carburettor
4   Adjust the throttle cable
5   Clean the spark plug and check the electrode gap
6   Lubricate the contact breaker cam wick
7   Grease all stand pivots, handlebar levers and footrests
8   Lubricate all control cables
9   Lubricate the speedometer cable
10  Check the steering head bearings for play
11  Examine the wheels and check for wear in the bearings
12  Adjust the brakes and check the degree of wear

### Four monthly or every 3700 miles (6000 km)

1   Decarbonize the cylinder head, barrel and exhaust system
2   Adjust and bleed the oil pump
3   Clean the tap fuel filter
4   Examine the fuel feed pipe for splitting and deterioration
5   Renew the spark plug
6   Reset the contact breaker gap and check the timing

# ROUTINE MAINTENANCE GUIDE

grease

High melting point grease

Lithium base grease

SAE 10W/30 motor oil

| | | |
|---|---|---|
| | bearings | |
| 7 | Swinging arm pivot shaft | As required |
| 8 | Pivot points | As required |
| 9 | Control cables | As required |

7  Renew the front fork oil
8  Grease the steering head bearing
9  Lubricate the swinging arm pivot
10 Examine and lubricate the wheel bearings
11 Lubricate the speedometer drive gear
12 Lubricate the brake cam shaft

Chain adjustment

**Final drive chain check and adjustment**

1  Split pin
2  Castellated nut
3  Adjusting bolt
4  Alignment marks

ROG HEALING  H 12295

Haynes ®

THE BOOK 800

# Spanner size comparison

| Jaw gap (in) | Spanner size | Jaw gap (in) | Spanner size |
|---|---|---|---|
| 0.250 | $\frac{1}{4}$ in AF | 0.945 | 24 mm |
| 0.276 | 7 mm | 1.000 | 1 in AF |
| 0.313 | $\frac{5}{16}$ in AF | 1.010 | $\frac{9}{16}$ in Whitworth; $\frac{5}{8}$ in BSF |
| 0.315 | 8 mm | 1.024 | 26 mm |
| 0.344 | $\frac{11}{32}$ in AF; $\frac{1}{8}$ in Whitworth | 1.063 | $1\frac{1}{16}$ in AF; 27 mm |
| 0.354 | 9 mm | 1.100 | $\frac{5}{8}$ in Whitworth; $\frac{11}{16}$ in BSF |
| 0.375 | $\frac{3}{8}$ in AF | 1.125 | $1\frac{1}{8}$ in AF |
| 0.394 | 10 mm | 1.181 | 30 mm |
| 0.433 | 11 mm | 1.200 | $\frac{11}{16}$ in Whitworth; $\frac{3}{4}$ in BSF |
| 0.438 | $\frac{7}{16}$ in AF | 1.250 | $1\frac{1}{4}$ in AF |
| 0.445 | $\frac{3}{8}$ in Whitworth; $\frac{1}{4}$ in BSF | 1.260 | 32 mm |
| 0.472 | 12 mm | 1.300 | $\frac{3}{4}$ in Whitworth; $\frac{7}{8}$ in BSF |
| 0.500 | $\frac{1}{2}$ in AF | 1.313 | $1\frac{5}{16}$ in AF |
| 0.512 | 13 mm | 1.390 | $\frac{13}{16}$ in Whitworth; $\frac{15}{16}$ in BSF |
| 0.525 | $\frac{1}{4}$ in Whitworth; $\frac{5}{16}$ in BSF | 1.417 | 36 mm |
| 0.551 | 14 mm | 1.438 | $1\frac{7}{16}$ in AF |
| 0.563 | $\frac{9}{16}$ in AF | 1.480 | $\frac{7}{8}$ in Whitworth; 1 in BSF |
| 0.591 | 15 mm | 1.500 | $1\frac{1}{2}$ in AF |
| 0.600 | $\frac{5}{16}$ in Whitworth; $\frac{3}{8}$ in BSF | 1.575 | 40 mm; $\frac{15}{16}$ in Whitworth |
| 0.625 | $\frac{5}{8}$ in AF | 1.614 | 41 mm |
| 0.630 | 16 mm | 1.625 | $1\frac{5}{8}$ in AF |
| 0.669 | 17 mm | 1.670 | 1 in Whitworth; $1\frac{1}{8}$ in BSF |
| 0.686 | $\frac{11}{16}$ in AF | 1.688 | $1\frac{11}{16}$ in AF |
| 0.709 | 18 mm | 1.811 | 46 mm |
| 0.710 | $\frac{3}{8}$ in Whitworth; $\frac{7}{16}$ in BSF | 1.813 | $1\frac{13}{16}$ in AF |
| 0.748 | 19 mm | 1.860 | $1\frac{1}{8}$ in Whitworth; $1\frac{1}{4}$ in BSF |
| 0.750 | $\frac{3}{4}$ in AF | 1.875 | $1\frac{7}{8}$ in AF |
| 0.813 | $\frac{13}{16}$ in AF | 1.969 | 50 mm |
| 0.820 | $\frac{7}{16}$ in Whitworth; $\frac{1}{2}$ in BSF | 2.000 | 2 in AF |
| 0.866 | 22 mm | 2.050 | $1\frac{1}{4}$ in Whitworth; $1\frac{3}{8}$ in BSF |
| 0.875 | $\frac{7}{8}$ in AF | 2.165 | 55 mm |
| 0.920 | $\frac{1}{2}$ in Whitworth; $\frac{9}{16}$ in BSF | 2.362 | 60 mm |
| 0.938 | $\frac{15}{16}$ in AF | | |

# Standard torque settings

Specific torque settings will be found at the end of the specifications section of each chapter. Where no figure is given, bolts should be secured according to the table below.

| Fastener type (thread diameter) | kgf m | lbf ft |
|---|---|---|
| 5mm bolt or nut | 0.45 – 0.6 | 3.5 – 4.5 |
| 6 mm bolt or nut | 0.8 – 1.2 | 6 – 9 |
| 8 mm bolt or nut | 1.8 – 2.5 | 13 – 18 |
| 10 mm bolt or nut | 3.0 – 4.0 | 22 – 29 |
| 12 mm bolt or nut | 5.0 – 6.0 | 36 – 43 |
| 5 mm screw | 0.35 – 0.5 | 2.5 – 3.6 |
| 6 mm screw | 0.7 – 1.1 | 5 – 8 |
| 6 mm flange bolt | 1.0 – 1.4 | 7 – 10 |
| 8 mm flange bolt | 2.4 – 3.0 | 17 – 22 |
| 10 mm flange bolt | 3.0 – 4.0 | 22 – 29 |

# Choosing and fitting accessories

The range of accessories available to the modern motorcyclist is almost as varied and bewildering as the range of motorcycles. This Section is intended to help the owner in choosing the correct equipment for his needs and to avoid some of the mistakes made by many riders when adding accessories to their machines. It will be evident that the Section can only cover the subject in the most general terms and so it is recommended that the owner, having decided that he wants to fit, for example, a luggage rack or carrier, seeks the advice of several local dealers and the owners of similar machines. This will give a good idea of what makes of carrier are easily available, and at what price. Talking to other owners will give some insight into the drawbacks or good points of any one make. A walk round the motorcycles in car parks or outside a dealer will often reveal the same sort of information.

The first priority when choosing accessories is to assess exactly what one needs. It is, for example, pointless to buy a large heavy-duty carrier which is designed to take the weight of fully laden panniers and topbox when all you need is a place to strap on a set of waterproofs and a lunchbox when going to work. Many accessory manufacturers have ranges of equipment to cater for the individual needs of different riders and this point should be borne in mind when looking through a dealer's catalogues. Having decided exactly what is required and the use to which the accessories are going to be put, the owner will need a few hints on what to look for when making the final choice. To this end the Section is now sub-divided to cover the more popular accessories fitted. Note that it is in no way a customizing guide, but merely seeks to outline the practical considerations to be taken into account when adding aftermarket equipment to a motorcycle.

## Fairings and windscreens

A fairing is possibly the single, most expensive, aftermarket item to be fitted to any motorcycle and, therefore, requires the most thought before purchase. Fairings can be divided into two main groups: front fork mounted handlebar fairings and windscreens, and frame mounted fairings.

The first group, the front fork mounted fairings, are becoming far more popular than was once the case, as they offer several advantages over the second group. Front fork mounted fairings generally are much easier and quicker to fit, involve less modification to the motorcycle, do not as a rule restrict the steering lock, permit a wider selection of handlebar styles to be used, and offer adequate protection for much less money than the frame mounted type. They are also lighter, can be swapped easily between different motorcycles, and are available in a much greater variety of styles. Their main disadvantages are that they do not offer as much weather protection as the frame mounted types, rarely offer any storage space, and, if poorly fitted or naturally incompatible, can have an adverse effect on the stability of the motorcycle.

The second group, the frame mounted fairings, are secured so rigidly to the main frame of the motorcycle that they can offer a substantial amount of protection to motorcycle and rider in the event of a crash. They offer almost complete protection from the weather and, if double-skinned in construction, can provide a great deal of useful storage space. The feeling of peace, quiet and complete relaxation encountered when riding behind a good full fairing has to be experienced to be believed. For this reason full fairings are considered essential by most touring motorcyclists and by many people who ride all year round. The main disadvantages of this type are that fitting can take a long time, often involving removal or modification of standard motorcycle components, they restrict the steering lock and they can add up to about 40 lb to the weight of the machine. They do not usually affect the stability of the machine to any great extent once the front tyre pressure and suspension have been adjusted to compensate for the extra weight, but can be affected by sidewinds.

The first thing to look for when purchasing a fairing is the quality of the fittings. A good fairing will have strong, substantial brackets constructed from heavy-gauge tubing; the brackets must be shaped to fit the frame or forks evenly so that the minimum of stress is imposed on the assembly when it is bolted down. The brackets should be properly painted or finished – a nylon coating being the favourite of the better manufacturers – the nuts and bolts provided should be of the same thread and size standard as is used on the motorcycle and be properly plated. Look also for shakeproof locking nuts or locking washers to ensure that everything remains securely tightened down. The fairing shell is generally made from one of two materials: fibreglass or ABS plastic. Both have their advantages and disadvantages, but the main consideration for the owner is that fibreglass is much easier to repair in the event of damage occurring to the fairing. Whichever material is used, check that it is properly finished inside as well as out, that the edges are protected by beading and that the fairing shell is insulated from vibration by the use of rubber grommets at all mounting points. Also be careful to check that the windscreen is retained by plastic bolts which will snap on impact so that the windscreen will break away and not cause personal injury in the event of an accident.

Having purchased your fairing or windscreen, read the manufacturer's fitting instructions very carefully and check that you have all the necessary brackets and fittings. Ensure that the mounting brackets are located correctly and bolted down securely. Note that some manufacturers use hose clamps to retain the mounting brackets; these should be discarded as they are convenient to use but not strong enough for the task. Stronger clamps should be substituted; car exhaust pipe clamps of suitable size would be a good alternative. Ensure that the front forks can turn through the full steering lock available without fouling the fairing. With many types of frame-mounted fairing the handlebars will have to be altered or a different type fitted and the steering lock will be restricted by stops provided with the fittings. Also check that the fairing does not foul the front wheel or mudguard, in any steering position, under full fork compression. Re-route any cables, brake pipes or electrical wiring which may snag on the fairing and take great care to protect all electrical connections, using insulating tape. If the manufacturer's instructions are followed carefully at every stage no serious problems should be encountered. Remember that hydraulic pipes that have been disconnected must be carefully re-tightened and the hydraulic system purged of air bubbles by bleeding.

Two things will become immediately apparent when taking a motorcycle on the road for the first time with a fairing – the first is the tendency to underestimate the road speed because of the lack of wind pressure on the body. This must be very carefully watched until one has grown accustomed to riding behind the fairing. The second thing is the alarming increase in engine noise which is an unfortunate but inevitable by-product of fitting any type of fairing or windscreen, and is caused by normal engine noise being reflected, and in some cases amplified, by the flat surface of the fairing.

## Luggage racks or carriers

Carriers are possibly the commonest item to be fitted to modern motorcycles. They vary enormously in size, carrying capacity, and durability. When selecting a carrier, always look for one which is made specifically for your machine and which is bolted on with as few separate brackets as possible. The universal-type carrier, with its mass of brackets and adaptor pieces, will generally prove too weak to be of any real use. A good carrier should bolt to the main frame, generally using the two suspension unit top mountings and a mudguard mounting bolt as attachment points, and have its luggage platform as low and as far forward as possible to minimise the effect of any load on the machine's stability. Look for good quality, heavy gauge tubing, good welding and good finish. Also ensure that the carrier does not prevent opening of the seat, sidepanels or tail compartment, as appropriate. When using a carrier, be very careful not to overload it. Excessive weight placed so high and so far to the rear of any motorcycle will have an adverse effect on the machine's steering and stability.

## Luggage

Motorcycle luggage can be grouped under two headings: soft and hard. Both types are available in many sizes and styles and have advantages and disadvantages in use.

Soft luggage is now becoming very popular because of its lower cost and its versatility. Whether in the form of tankbags, panniers, or strap-on bags, soft luggage requires in general no brackets and no modification to the motorcycle. Equipment can be swapped easily from one motorcycle to another and can be fitted and removed in seconds. Awkwardly shaped loads can easily be carried. The disadvantages of soft luggage are that the contents cannot be secure against the casual thief, very little protection is afforded in the event of a crash, and waterproofing is generally poor. Also, in the case of panniers, carrying capacity is restricted to approximately 10 lb, although this amount will vary considerably depending on the manufacturer's recommendation. When purchasing soft luggage, look for good quality material, generally vinyl or nylon, with strong, well-stitched attachment points. It is always useful to have separate pockets, especially on tank bags, for items which will be needed on the journey. When purchasing a tank bag, look for one which has a separate, well-padded, base. This will protect the tank's paintwork and permit easy access to the filler cap at petrol stations.

Hard luggage is confined to two types: panniers, and top boxes or tail trunks. Most hard luggage manufacturers produce matching sets of these items, the basis of which is generally that manufacturer's own heavy-duty luggage rack. Variations on this theme occur in the form of separate frames for the better quality panniers, fixed or quickly-detachable luggage, and in size and carrying capacity. Hard luggage offers a reasonable degree of security against theft and good protection against weather and accident damage. Carrying capacity is greater than that of soft luggage, around 15 – 20 lb in the case of panniers, although top boxes should never be loaded as much as their apparent capacity might imply. A top box should only be used for lightweight items, because one that is heavily laden can have a serious effect on the stability of the machine. When purchasing hard luggage look for the same good points as mentioned under fairings and windscreens, ie good quality mounting brackets and fittings, and well finished fibreglass or ABS plastic cases. Again as with fairings, always purchase luggage made specifically for your motorcycle, using as few separate brackets as possible, to ensure that everything remains securely bolted in place. When fitting hard luggage, be careful to check that the rear suspension and brake operation will not be impaired in any way and remember that many pannier kits require re-siting of the indicators. Remember also that a non-standard exhaust system may make fitting extremely difficult.

## Handlebars

The occupation of fitting alternative types of handlebar is extremely popular with modern motorcyclists, whose motives may vary from the purely practical, wishing to improve the comfort of their machines, to the purely aesthetic, where form is more important than function. Whatever the reason, there are several considerations to be borne in mind when changing the handlebars of your machine. If fitting lower bars, check carefully that the switches and cables do not foul the petrol tank on full lock and that the surplus lengths of cable, brake

pipe, and electrical wiring are smoothly and tidily disposed of. Avoid tight kinks in cable or brake pipes which will produce stiff controls or the premature and disastrous failure of an overstressed component. If necessary, remove the petrol tank and re-route the cable from the engine/gearbox unit upwards, ensuring smooth gentle curves are produced. In extreme cases, it will be necessary to purchase a shorter brake pipe to overcome this problem. In the case of higher handlebars than standard it will almost certainly be necessary to purchase extended cables and brake pipes. Fortunately, many standard motor cycles have a custom version which will be equipped with higher handlebars and, therefore, factory-built extended components will be available from your local dealer. It is not usually necessary to extend electrical wiring, as switch clusters may be used on several different motorcycles, some being custom versions. This point should be borne in mind however when fitting extremely high or wide handlebars.

When fitting different types of handlebar, ensure that the mounting clamps are correctly tightened to the manufacturer's specifications and that cables and wiring, as previously mentioned, have smooth easy runs and do not snag on any part of the motorcycle throughout the full steering lock. Ensure that the fluid level in the front brake master cylinder remains level to avoid any chance of air entering the hydraulic system. Also check that the cables are adjusted correctly and that all handlebar controls operate correctly and can be easily reached when riding.

## Crashbars

Crashbars, also known as engine protector bars, engine guards, or case savers, are extremely useful items of equipment which can contribute protection to the machine's structure if a crash occurs. They do not, as has been inferred in the US, prevent the rider from crashing, or necessarily prevent rider injury should a crash occur.

It is recommended that only the smaller, neater, engine protector type of crashbar is considered. This type will offer protection while restricting, as little as is possible, access to the engine and the machine's ground clearance. The crashbars should be designed for use specifically on your machine, and should be constructed of heavy-gauge tubing with strong, integral mounting brackets. Where possible, they should bolt to a strong lug on the frame, usually at the engine mounting bolts.

The alternative type of crashbar is the larger cage type. This type is not recommended in spite of their appearance which promises some protection to the rider as well as to the machine. The larger amount of leverage imposed by the size of this type of crashbar increases the risk of severe frame damage in the event of an accident. This type also decreases the machine's ground clearance and restricts access to the engine. The amount of protection afforded the rider is open to some doubt as the design is based on the premise that the rider will stay in the normally seated position during an accident, and the crash bar structure will not itself fail. Neither result can in any way be guaranteed.

As a general rule, always purchase the best, ie usually the most expensive, set of crashbars you can afford. The investment will be repaid by minimising the amount of damage incurred, should the machine be involved in an accident. Finally, avoid the universal type of crashbar. This should be regarded only as a last resort to be used if no alternative exists. With its usual multitude of separate brackets and spacers, the universal crashbar is far too weak in design and construction to be of any practical value.

## Exhaust systems

The fitting of aftermarket exhaust systems is another extremely popular pastime amongst motorcyclists. The usual motive is to gain more performance from the engine but other considerations are to gain more ground clearance, to lose weight from the motorcycle, to obtain a more distinctive exhaust note or to find a cheaper alternative to the manufacturer's original equipment exhaust system. Original equipment exhaust systems often cost more and may well have a relatively short life. It should be noted that it is rare for an aftermarket exhaust system alone to give a noticeable increase in the engine's power output. Modern motorcycles are designed to give the highest power output possible allowing for factors such as quietness, fuel economy, spread of power, and long-term reliability. If there were a magic formula which allowed the exhaust system to produce more power without affecting these other considerations you can be sure that the manufacturers, with their large research and development facilities, would have found it and made use of it. Performance increases of a worthwhile and noticeable nature only come from well-tried and properly matched modifications to the entire engine, from the air filter, through the carburettors, port timing or camshaft and valve design, combustion chamber shape, compression ratio, and the exhaust system. Such modifications are well outside the scope of this manual but interested owners might refer to the 'Piper Tuning Manual' produced by the publisher of this manual; this book goes into the whole subject in great detail.

Whatever your motive for wishing to fit an alternative exhaust system, be sure to seek expert advice before doing so. Changes to the carburettor jetting will almost certainly be required for which you must consult the exhaust system manufacturer. If he cannot supply adequately specific information it is reasonable to assume that insufficient development work has been carried out, and that particular make should be avoided. Other factors to be borne in mind are whether the exhaust system allows the use of both centre and side stands, whether it allows sufficient access to permit oil and filter changing and whether modifications are necessary to the standard exhaust system. Many two-stroke expansion chamber systems require the use of the standard exhaust pipe; this is all very well if the standard exhaust pipe and silencer are separate units but can cause problems if the two, as with so many modern two-strokes, are a one-piece unit. While the exhaust pipe can be removed easily by means of a hacksaw it is not so easy to refit the original silencer should you at any time wish to return the machine to standard trim. The same applies to several four-stroke systems.

On the subject of the finish of aftermarket exhausts, avoid black-painted systems unless you enjoy painting. As any trail-bike owner will tell you, rust has a great affinity for black exhausts and re-painting or rust removal becomes a task which must be carried out with monotonous regularity. A bright chrome finish is, as a general rule, a far better proposition as it is much easier to keep clean and to prevent rusting. Although the general finish of aftermarket exhaust systems is not always up to the standard of the original equipment the lower cost of such systems does at least reflect this fact.

When fitting an alternative system always purchase a full set of new exhaust gaskets, to prevent leaks. Fit the exhaust first to the cylinder head or barrel, as appropriate, tightening the retaining nuts or bolts by hand only and then line up the exhaust rear mountings. If the new system is a one-piece unit and the rear mountings do not line up exactly, spacers must be fabricated to take up the difference. Do not force the system into place as the stress thus imposed will rapidly cause cracks and splits to appear. Once all the mountings are loosely fixed, tighten the retaining nuts or bolts securely, being careful not to overtighten them. Where the motorcycle manufacturer's torque settings are available, these should be used. Do not forget to carry out any carburation changes recommended by the exhaust system's manufacturer.

## Electrical equipment

The vast range of electrical equipment available to motorcyclists is so large and so diverse that only the most general outline can be given here. Electrical accessories vary from electric ignition kits fitted to replace contact breaker points, to additional lighting at the front and rear, more powerful horns, various instruments and gauges, clocks, anti-theft systems, heated clothing, CB radios, radio-cassette players, and intercom systems, to name but a few of the more popular items of equipment.

As will be evident, it would require a separate manual to cover this subject alone and this section is therefore restricted to outlining a few basic rules which must be borne in mind when fitting electrical equipment. The first consideration is whether your machine's electrical system has enough reserve capacity to cope with the added demand of the accessories you wish to fit. The motorcycle's manufacturer or importer should be able to furnish this sort of information and may also be able to offer advice on uprating the electrical system. Failing this, a good dealer or the accessory manufacturer may be able to help. In some cases, more powerful generator components may be available, perhaps from another motorcycle in the manufacturer's range. The second consideration is the legal requirements in force in your area. The local police may be prepared to help with this point. In the UK for example, there are strict regulations governing the position and use of auxiliary riding lamps and fog lamps.

When fitting electrical equipment always disconnect the battery first to prevent the risk of a short-circuit, and be careful to ensure that all connections are properly made and that they are waterproof. Remember that many electrical accessories are designed primarily for use in cars and that they cannot easily withstand the exposure to vibration and to the weather. Delicate components must be rubber-mounted to insulate them from vibration, and sealed carefully to prevent the entry of rainwater and dirt. Be careful to follow exactly the accessory manufacturer's instructions in conjunction with the wiring diagram at the back of this manual.

## Accessories – general

Accessories fitted to your motorcycle will rapidly deteriorate if not cared for. Regular washing and polishing will maintain the finish and will provide an opportunity to check that all mounting bolts and nuts are securely fastened. Any signs of chafing or wear should be watched for, and the cause cured as soon as possible before serious damage occurs.

As a general rule, do not expect the re-sale value of your motorcycle to increase by an amount proportional to the amount of money and effort put into fitting accessories. It is usually the case that an absolutely standard motorcycle will sell more easily at a better price than one that has been modified. If you are in the habit of exchanging your machine for another at frequent intervals, this factor should be borne in mind to avoid loss of money.

# Fault diagnosis

**Contents**

## 1   Introduction

This Section provides an easy reference-guide to the more common ailments that are likely to afflict your machine. Obviously, the opportunities are almost limitless for faults to occur as a result of obscure failures, and to try and cover all eventualities would require a book. Indeed, a number have been written on the subject.

Successful fault diagnosis is not a mysterious 'black art' but the application of a bit of knowledge combined with a systematic and logical approach to the problem. Approach any fault diagnosis by first accurately identifying the symptom and then checking through the list of possibile causes, starting with the simplest or most obvious and progressing in stages to the most complex. Take nothing for granted, but above all apply liberal quantities of common sense.

The main symptom of a fault is given in the text as a major heading below which are listed, as Sections headings, the various systems or areas which may contain the fault. Details of each possible cause for a fault and the remedial action to be taken are given, in brief, in the paragraphs below each Section heading. Further information should be sought in the relevant Chapter.


## *Engine does not start when turned over*

## 2   No fuel flow to carburettor

● Fuel tank empty or level too low. Check that the tap is turned to 'On' or 'Reserve' position as required. If in doubt, prise off the fuel feed pipe at the carburettor end and check that fuel runs from pipe when the tap is turned on.
● Tank filler cap vent obstructed. This can prevent fuel from flowing into the carburettor float bowl bcause air cannot enter the fuel tank to replace it. The problem is more likely to appear when the machine is being ridden. Check by listening close to the filler cap and releasing it. A hissing noise indicates that a blockage is present. Remove the cap and clear the vent hole with wire or by using an air line from the inside of the cap.
● Fuel tap or filter blocked. Blockage may be due to accumulation of rust or paint flakes from the tank's inner surface or of foreign matter from contaminated fuel. Remove the tap and clean it and the filter. Look also for water droplets in the fuel.
● Fuel line blocked. Blockage of the fuel line is more likely to result from a kink in the line rather than the accumulation of debris.


## 3   Fuel not reaching cylinder

● Float chamber not filling. Caused by float needle or floats sticking in up position. This may occur after the machine has been left standing for an extended length of time allowing the fuel to evaporate. When this occurs a gummy residue is often left which hardens to a varnish-like substance. This condition may be worsened by corrosion and crystalline deposits produced prior to the total evaporation of contaminated fuel. Sticking of the float needle may also be caused by wear. In any case removal of the float chamber will be necessary for inspection and cleaning.
● Blockage in starting circuit, slow running circuit or jets. Blockage of these items may be attributable to debris from the fuel tank by-passing the filter system or to gumming up as described in paragraph 1. Water droplets in the fuel will also block jets and passages. The carburettor should be dismantled for cleaning.
● Fuel level too low. The fuel level in the float chamber is controlled by float height. The fuel level may increase with wear or damage but will never reduce, thus a low fuel level is an inherent rather than developing condition. Check the float height, renewing the float or needle if required.


## 4   Engine flooding

● Float valve needle worn or stuck open. A piece of rust or other debris can prevent correct seating of the needle against the valve seat thereby permitting an uncontrolled flow of fuel. Similarly, a worn needle or needle seat will prevent valve closure. Dismantle the carburettor float bowl for cleaning and, if necessary, renewal of the worn components.
● Fuel level too high. The fuel level is controlled by the float height which may increase due to wear of the float needle, pivot pin or operating tang. Check the float height, and make any necessary adjustments. A leaking float will cause an increase in fuel level, and thus should be renewed.
● Cold starting mechanism. Check the choke (starter mechanism) for correct operation. If the mechanism jams in the 'On' position subsequent starting of a hot engine will be difficult.
● Blocked air filter. A badly restricted air filter will cause flooding. Check the filter and clean or renew as required. A collapsed inlet hose will have a similar effect. Check that the air filter inlet has not become blocked by a rag or similar item.


## 5   No spark at plug

● Ignition switch not on.
● Engine stop switch off.
● Spark plug dirty, oiled or 'whiskered'. Because the induction mixture of a two-stroke engine is inclined to be of a rather oily nature it is comparatively easy to foul the plug electrodes, especially where there have been repeated attempts to start the engine. A machine used for short journeys will be more prone to fouling because the engine may never reach full operating temperature, and the deposits will not burn off. On rare occasions a change of plug grade may be required but the advice of a dealer should be sought before making such a change. 'Whiskering' is a comparatively rare occurrence on modern machines but may be encountered where pre-mixed petrol and oil (petroil) lubrication is employed. An electrode deposit in the form of a barely visible filament across the plug electrodes can short circuit the plug and prevent its sparking. On all two-stroke machines it is a sound precaution to carry a new spare spark plug for substitution in the event of fouling problems.
● Spark plug failure. Clean the spark plug thoroughly and reset the electrode gap. Refer to the spark plug section and the colour condition guide in Chapter 3. If the spark plug shorts internally or has sustained visible damage to the electrodes, core or ceramic insulator it should be renewed. On rare occasions a plug that appears to spark vigorously will fail to do so when refitted to the engine and subjected to the compression pressure in the cylinder.
● Spark plug cap or high tension (HT) lead faulty. Check condition and security. Replace if deterioration is evident. Most spark plugs have an internal resistor designed to inhibit electrical interference with radio and television sets. On rare occasions the resistor may break down, thus preventing sparking. If this is suspected, fit a new cap as a precaution.
● Spark plug cap loose. Check that the spark plug cap fits securely over the plug and, where fitted, the screwed terminal on the plug end is secure.
● Shorting due to moisture. Certain parts of the ignition system are susceptible to shorting when the machine is ridden or parked in wet weather. Check particularly the area from the spark plug cap back to the ignition coil. A water dispersant spray may be used to dry out waterlogged components. Recurrence of the problem can be prevented by using an ignition sealant spray after drying out and cleaning.
● Ignition or stop switch shorted. May be caused by water corrosion or wear. Water dispersant and contact cleaning sprays may be used. If this fails to overcome the problem dismantling and visual inspection of the switches will be required.
● Shorting or open circuit in wiring. Failure in any wire connecting any of the ignition components will cause ignition malfunction. Check also that all connections are clean, dry and tight.
● Ignition coil failure. Check the coil, referring to Chapter 3.
● Capacitor (condenser) failure. The capacitor may be checked most easily by substitution with a replacement item. Blackened contact breaker points indicate capacitor malfunction but this may not always occur.
● Contact breaker points pitted, burned or closed up. Check the contact breaker points, referring to Chapter 3. Check also that the low tension leads at the contact breaker are secure and not shorting out.

## 6 Weak spark at plug

● Feeble sparking at the plug may be caused by any of the faults mentioned in the preceding Section other than those items in the first two paragraphs. Check first the contact breaker assembly and the spark plug, these being the most likely culprits.

## 7 Compression low

● Spark plug loose. This will be self-evident on inspection, and may be accompanied by a hissing noise when the engine is turned over. Remove the plug and check that the threads in the cylinder head are not damaged. Check also that the plug sealing washer is in good condition.
● Cylinder head gasket leaking. This condition is often accompanied by a high pitched squeak from around the cylinder head and oil loss, and may be caused by insufficiently tightened cylinder head fasteners, a warped cylinder head or mechanical failure of the gasket material. Re-torqueing the fasteners to the correct specification may seal the leak in some instances but if damage has occurred this course of action will provide, at best, only a temporary cure.
● Low crankcase compression. This can be caused by worn main bearings and seals and will upset the incoming fuel/air mixture. A good seal in these areas is essential on any two-stroke engine.
● Piston rings sticking or broken. Sticking of the piston rings may be caused by seizure due to lack of lubrication or overheating as a result of poor carburation or incorrect fuel type. Gumming of the rings may result from lack of use, or carbon deposits in the ring grooves. Broken rings result from over-revving, over-heating or general wear. In either case a top-end overhaul will be required.

## Engine stalls after starting

### 8 General causes

● Improper cold start mechanism operation. Check that the operating controls function smoothly and, where applicable, are correctly adjusted. A cold engine may not require application of an enriched mixture to start initially but may baulk without choke once firing. Likewise a hot engine may start with an enriched mixture but will stop almost immediately if the choke is inadvertently in operation.
● Ignition malfunction. See Section 9. Weak spark at plug.
● Carburettor incorrectly adjusted. Maladjustment of the mixture strength or idle speed may cause the engine to stop immediately after starting. See Routine Maintenance.
● Fuel contamination. Check for filter blockage by debris or water which reduces, but does not completely stop, fuel flow, or blockage of the slow speed circuit in the carburettor by the same agents. If water is present it can often be seen as droplets in the bottom of the float bowl. Clean the filter and, where water is in evidence, drain and flush the fuel tank and float bowl.
● Intake air leak. Check for security of the carburettor mounting and hose connections, and for cracks or splits in the hoses. Check also that the carburettor top is secure and that the vacuum gauge adaptor plug (where fitted) is tight.
● Air filter blocked or omitted. A blocked filter will cause an over-rich mixture; the omission of a filter will cause an excessively weak mixture. Both conditions will have a detrimental effect on carburation. Clean or renew the filter as necessary.
● Fuel filler cap air vent blocked. Usually caused by dirt or water. Clean the vent orifice.
● Choked exhaust system. Caused by excessive carbon build-up in the system, particularly around the silencer baffles. In many cases these can be detached for cleaning, though mopeds have one-piece systems which require a rather different approach. Refer to Routine Maintenance for further information.
● Excessive carbon build-up in the engine. This can result from failure to decarbonise the engine at the specified interval or through excessive oil consumption. On pump-fed engines check pump adjustment.

## Poor running at idle and low speed

### 9 Weak spark at plug or erratic firing

● Battery voltage low. In certain conditions low battery charge, especially when coupled with a badly sulphated battery, may result in misifirng. If the battery is in good general condition it should be recharged; an old battery suffering from sulphated plates should be renewed.
● Spark plug fouled, faulty or incorrectly adjusted. See Section 4 or refer to Routine Maintenance.
● Spark plug cap or high tension lead shorting. Check the condition of both these items ensuring that they are in good condition and dry and that the cap is fitted correctly.
● Spark plug type incorrect. Fit plug of correct type and heat range as given in Specifications. In certain conditions a plug of hotter or colder type may be required for normal running.
● Contact breaker points pitted, burned or closed-up. Check the contact breaker assembly, referring to Chapter 3.
● Ignition timing incorrect. Check the ignition timing statically.
● Faulty ignition coil. Partial failure of the coil internal insulation will diminish the performance of the coil. No repair is possible, a new component must be fitted.
● Faulty capacitor (condenser). A failure of the capacitor will cause blackening of the contact breaker point faces and will allow excessive sparking at the points. A faulty capacitor may best be checked by substitution of a serviceable replacement item.
● Defective flywheel generator ignition source. Refer to Chapter 3 for further details on test procedures.

### 10 Fuel/air mixture incorrect

● Intake air leak. Check carburettor mountings and air cleaner hoses for security and signs of splitting. Ensure that carburettor top is tight and that the vacuum gauge take-off plug (where fitted) is tight.
● Mixture strength incorrect. Adjust slow running mixture strength using pilot adjustment screw.
● Pilot jet or slow running circuit blocked. The carburettor should be removed and dismantled for thorough cleaning. Blow through all jets and air passages with compressed air to clear obstructions.
● Air cleaner clogged or omitted. Clean or fit air cleaner element as necessary. Check also that the element and air filter cover are correctly seated.
● Cold start mechanism in operation. Check that the choke has not been left on inadvertently and the operation is correct.
● Fuel level too high or too low. Check the float height, renewing float or needle if required. See Section 3 or 4.
● Fuel tank air vent obstructed. Obstructions usually caused by dirt or water. Clean vent orifice.

### 11 Compression low

● See Section 7.

## Acceleration poor

### 12 General causes

● All items as for previous Section.
● Choked air filter. Failure to keep the air filter element clean will allow the build-up of dirt with proportional loss of performance. In extreme cases of neglect acceleration will suffer.
● Choked exhaust system. This can result from failure to remove accumulations of carbon from the silencer baffles at the prescribed intervals. The increased back pressure will make the machine noticeably sluggish. Refer to Routine Maintenance for further information on decarbonisation.

● Excessive carbon build-up in the engine. This can result from failure to decarbonise the engine at the specified interval or through excessive oil consumption. On pump-fed engines check pump adjustment.
● Ignition timing incorrect. Check the contact breaker gap and set within the prescribed range ensuring that the ignition timing is correct. If the contact breaker assembly is worn it may prove impossible to get the gap and timing settings to coincide, necessitating renewal.
● Carburation fault. See Section 10.
● Mechanical resistance. Check that the brakes are not binding. On small machines in particular note that the increased rolling resistance caused by under-inflated tyres may impede acceleration.

## Poor running or lack of power at high speeds

### 13 Weak spark at plug or erratic firing

● All items as for Section 9.
● HT lead insulation failure. Insulation failure of the HT lead and spark plug cap due to old age or damage can cause shorting when the engine is driven hard. This condition may be less noticeable, or not noticeable at all at lower engine speeds.

### 14 Fuel/air mixture incorrect

● All items as for Section 10, with the exception of items relative exclusively to low speed running.
● Main jet blocked. Debris from contaminated fuel, or from the fuel tank, and water in the fuel can block the main jet. Clean the fuel filter, the float bowl area, and if water is present, flush and refill the fuel tank.
● Main jet is the wrong size. The standard carburettor jetting is for sea level atmospheric pressure. For high altitudes, usually above 5000 ft, a smaller main jet will be required.
● Jet needle and needle jet worn. These can be renewed individually but should be renewed as a pair. Renewal of both items requires partial dismantling of the carburettor.
● Air bleed holes blocked. Dismantle carburettor and use compressed air to blow out all air passages.
● Reduced fuel flow. A reduction in the maximum fuel flow from the fuel tank to the carburettor will cause fuel starvation, proportionate to the engine speed. Check for blockages through debris or a kinked fuel line.

### 15 Compression low

● See Section 7.

## Knocking or pinking

### 16 General causes

● Carbon build-up in combustion chamber. After high mileages have been covered large accumulations of carbon may occur. This may glow red hot and cause premature ignition of the fuel/air mixture, in advance of normal firing by the spark plug. Cylinder head removal will be required to allow inspection and cleaning.
● Fuel incorrect. A low grade fuel, or one of poor quality may result in compression induced detonation of the fuel resulting in knocking and pinking noises. Old fuel can cause similar problems. A too highly leaded fuel will reduce detonation but will accelerate deposit formation in the combustion chamber and may lead to early pre-ignition as described in item 1.
● Spark plug heat range incorrect. Uncontrolled pre-ignition can result from the use of a spark plug the heat range of which is too hot.
● Weak mixture. Overheating of the engine due to a weak mixture can result in pre-ignition occurring where it would not occur when engine temperature was within normal limits. Maladjustment, blocked jets or passages and air leaks can cause this condition.

## Overheating

### 17 Firing incorrect

● Spark plug fouled, defective or maladjusted. See Section 5.
● Spark plug type incorrect. Refer to the Specifications and ensure that the correct plug type is fitted.
● Incorrect ignition timing. Timing that is far too much advanced or far too much retarded will cause overheating. Check the ignition timing is correct.

### 18 Fuel/air mixture incorrect

● Slow speed mixture strength incorrect. Adjust pilot air screw.
● Main jet wrong size. The carburettor is jetted for sea level atmospheric conditions. For high altitudes, usually above 5000 ft, a smaller main jet will be required.
● Air filter badly fitted or omitted. Check that the filter element is in place and that it and the air filter box cover are sealing correctly. Any leaks will cause a weak mixture.
● Induction air leaks. Check the security of the carburettor mountings and hose connections, and for cracks and splits in the hoses. Check also that the carburettor top is secure.
● Fuel level too low. See Section 3.
● Fuel tank filler cap air vent obstructed. Clear blockage.

### 19 Lubrication inadequate

● Oil pump settings incorrect. The oil pump settings are of great importance since the quantities of oil being injected are very small. Any variation in oil delivery will have a significant effect on the engine. Refer to Chapter 2 for further information.
● Oil tank empty or low. This will have disastrous consequences if left unnoticed. Check and replenish tank regularly.
● Transmission oil low or worn out. Check the level regularly and investigate any loss of oil. If the oil level drops with no sign of external leakage it is likely that the crankshaft main bearing oil seals are worn, allowing transmission oil to be drawn into the crankcase during induction.

### 20 Miscellaneous causes

● Engine fins clogged. A build-up of mud in the cylinder head and cylinder barrel cooling fins will decrease the cooling capabilities of the fins. Clean the fins as required.

## Clutch operating problems

### 21 Clutch slip

● No clutch lever play. Adjust clutch lever end play according to the procedure in Routine Maintenance.
● Friction plates worn or warped. Overhaul clutch assembly, replacing plates out of specification.
● Steel plates worn or warped. Overhaul clutch assembly, replacing plates out of specification.
● Clutch spring broken or worn. Old or heat-damaged (from slipping clutch) springs should be replaced with new ones.
● Clutch release not adjusted properly. See the adjustments section of Chapter 1.
● Clutch inner cable snagging. Caused by a frayed cable or kinked outer cable. Replace the cable with a new one. Repair of a frayed cable is not advised.
● Clutch release mechanism defective. Worn or damaged parts in the clutch release mechanism could include the shaft, cam, actuating arm or pivot. Replace parts as necessary.
● Clutch hub and outer drum worn. Severe indentation by the clutch plate tangs of the channels in the hub and drum will cause snagging of the plates preventing correct engagement. If this damage occurs, renewal of the worn components is required.

● Lubricant incorrect. Use of a transmission lubricant other than that specified may allow the plates to slip.

## 22 Clutch drag

● Clutch lever play excessive. Adjust lever at bars or at cable end if necessary.
● Clutch plates warped or damaged. This will cause a drag on the clutch, causing the machine to creep. Overhaul clutch assembly.
● Clutch spring tension uneven. Usually caused by a sagged or broken spring. Check and replace springs.
● Transmission oil deteriorated. Badly contaminated transmission oil and a heavy deposit of oil sludge on the plates will cause plate sticking. The oil recommended for this machine is of the detergent type, therefore it is unlikely that this problem will arise unless regular oil changes are neglected.
● Transmission oil viscosity too high. Drag in the plates will result from the use of an oil with too high a viscosity. In very cold weather clutch drag may occur until the engine has reached operating temperature.
● Clutch hub and outer drum worn. Indentation by the clutch plate tangs of the channels in the hub and drum will prevent easy plate disengagement. If the damage is light the affected areas may be dressed with a fine file. More pronounced damage will necessitate renewal of the components.
● Clutch housing seized to shaft. Lack of lubrication, severe wear or damage can cause the housing to seize to the shaft. Overhaul of the clutch, and perhaps the transmission, may be necessary to repair damage.
● Clutch release mechanism defective. Worn or damaged release mechanism parts can stick and fail to provide leverage. Overhaul clutch cover components.
● Loose clutch hub nut. Causes drum and hub misalignment, putting a drag on the engine. Engagement adjustment continually varies. Overhaul clutch assembly.

## *Gear selection problems*

## 23 Gear lever does not return

● Weak or broken centraliser spring. Renew the spring.
● Gearchange shaft bent or seized. Distortion of the gearchange shaft often occurs if the machine is dropped heavily on the gear lever. Provided that damage is not severe straightening of the shaft is permissible.

## 24 Gear selection difficult or impossible

● Clutch not disengaging fully. See Section 22.
● Gearchange shaft bent. This often occurs if the machine is dropped heavily on the gear lever. Straightening of the shaft is permissible if the damage is not too great.
● Gearchange arms, pawls or pins worn or damaged. Wear or breakage of any of these items may cause difficulty in selecting one or more gears. Overhaul the selector mechanism.
● Gearchange shaft centraliser spring maladjusted. This is often characterised by difficulties in changing up or down, but rarely in both directions. Adjust the centraliser anchor bolt as described in Chapter 1.
● Gearchange drum stopper cam or detent plunger damaged. Failure, rather than wear of these items may jam the drum thereby preventing gearchanging or causing false selection at high speed.
● Selector forks bent or seized. This can be caused by dropping the machine heavily on the gearchange lever or as a result of lack of lubrication. Though rare, bending of a shaft can result from a missed gearchange or false selection at high speed.
● Selector fork end and pin wear. Pronounced wear of these items and the grooves in the gearchange drum can lead to imprecise selection and, eventually, no selection. Renewal of the worn components will be required.
● Structural failure. Failure of any one component of the selector rod and change mechanism will result in improper or fouled gear selection.

## 25 Jumping out of gear

● Detent plunger assembly worn or damaged. Wear of the plunger and the cam with which it locates and breakage of the detent spring can cause imprecise gear selection resulting in jumping out of gear. Renew the damaged components.
● Gear pinion dogs worn or damaged. Rounding off the dog edges and the mating recesses in adjacent pinion can lead to jumping out of gear when under load. The gears should be inspected and renewed. Attempting to reprofile the dogs is not recommended.
● Selector forks, gearchange drum and pinion grooves worn. Extreme wear of these interconnected items can occur after high mileages especially when lubrication has been neglected. The worn components must be renewed.
● Gear pinions, bushes and shafts worn. Renew the worn components.
● Bent gearchange shaft. Often caused by dropping the machine on the gear lever.
● Gear pinion tooth broken. Chipped teeth are unlikely to cause jumping out of gear once the gear has been selected fully; a tooth which is completely broken off, however, may cause problems in this respect and in any event will cause transmission noise.

## 26 Overselection

● Pawl spring weak or broken. Renew the spring.
● Detent plunger worn or broken. Renew the damaged items.
● Stopper arm spring worn or broken. Renew the spring.
● Gearchange arm stop pads worn. Repairs can be made by welding and reprofiling with a file.
● Selector limiter claw components (where fitted) worn or damaged. Renew the damaged items.

## *Abnormal engine noise*

## 27 Knocking or pinking

● See Section 16.

## 28 Piston slap or rattling from cylinder

● Cylinder bore/piston clearance excessive. Resulting from wear, or partial seizure. This condition can often be heard as a high, rapid tapping noise when the engine is under little or no load, particularly when power is just beginning to be applied. Reboring to the next correct oversize should be carried out and a new oversize piston fitted.
● Connecting rod bent. This can be caused by over-revving, trying to start a very badly flooded engine (resulting in a hydraulic lock in the cylinder) or by earlier mechanical failure. Attempts at straightening a bent connecting rod from a high performance engine are not recommended. Careful inspection of the crankshaft should be made before renewing the damaged connecting rod.
● Gudgeon pin, piston boss bore or small-end bearing wear or seizure. Excess clearance or partial seizure between normal moving parts of these items can cause continuous or intermittent tapping noises. Rapid wear or seizure is caused by lubrication starvation.
● Piston rings worn, broken or sticking. Renew the rings after careful inspection of the piston and bore.

## 29 Other noises

● Big-end bearing wear. A pronounced knock from within the crankcase which worsens rapidly is indicative of big-end bearing failure as a result of extreme normal wear or lubrication failure. Remedial action in the form of a bottom end overhaul should be taken; continuing to run the engine will lead to further damage including the possibility of connecting rod breakage.
● Main bearing failure. Extreme normal wear or failure of the main bearings is characteristically accompanied by a rumble from the

crankcase and vibration felt through the frame and footrests. Renew the worn bearings and carry out a very careful examination of the crankshaft.

● Crankshaft excessively out of true. A bent crank may result from over-revving or damage from an upper cylinder component or gearbox failure. Damage can also result from dropping the machine on either crankshaft end. Straightening of the crankshaft is not be possible in normal circumstances; a replacement item should be fitted.

● Engine mounting loose. Tighten all the engine mounting nuts and bolts.

● Cylinder head gasket leaking. The noise most often associated with a leaking head gasket is a high pitched squeaking, although any other noise consistent with gas being forced out under pressure from a small orifice can also be emitted. Gasket leakage is often accompanied by oil seepage from around the mating joint or from the cylinder head holding down bolts and nuts. Leakage results from insufficient or uneven tightening of the cylinder head fasteners, or from random mechanical failure. Retightening to the correct torque figure will, at best, only provide a temporary cure. The gasket should be renewed at the earliest opportunity.

● Exhaust system leakage. Popping or crackling in the exhaust system, particularly when it occurs with the engine on the overrun, indicates a poor joint either at the cylinder port or at the exhaust pipe/silencer connection. Failure of the gasket or looseness of the clamp should be looked for.

## Abnormal transmission noise

### 30 Clutch noise

● Clutch outer drum/friction plate tang clearance excessive.
● Clutch outer drum/spacer clearance excessive.
● Clutch outer drum/thrust washer clearance excessive.
● Primary drive gear teeth worn or damaged.
● Clutch shock absorber assembly worn or damaged.

### 31 Transmission noise

● Bearing or bushes worn or damaged. Renew the affected components.
● Gear pinions worn or chipped. Renew the gear pinions.
● Metal chips jammed in gear teeth. This can occur when pieces of metal from any failed component are picked up by a meshing pinion. The condition will lead to rapid bearing wear or early gear failure.
● Engine/transmission oil level too low. Top up immediately to prevent damage to gearbox and engine.
● Gearchange mechanism worn or damaged. Wear or failure of certain items in the selection and change components can induce mis-selection of gears (see Section 24) where incipient engagement of more than one gear set is promoted. Remedial action, by the overhaul of the gearbox, should be taken without delay.
● Chain snagging on cases or cycle parts. A badly worn chain or one that is excessively loose may snag or smack against adjacent components.

## Exhaust smokes excessively

### 32 White/blue smoke (caused by oil burning)

● Cylinder cracked, worn or scored. These conditions may be caused by overheating, lack of lubrication, component failure or advanced normal wear. The cylinder barrel should be renewed and, if necessary, a new piston fitted.
● Oil pump settings incorrect. Check and reset the oil pump as described in Chapter 2.
● Crankshaft main bearing oil seals worn. Wear in the main bearing oil seals, often in conjunction with wear in the bearings themselves, can allow transmission oil to find its way into the crankcase and thence to the combustion chamber. This condition is often indicated by a mysterious drop in the transmission oil level with no sign of external leakage.

● Accumulated oil deposits in exhaust system. If the machine is used for short journeys only it is possible for the oil residue in the exhaust gases to condense in the relatively cool silencer. If the machine is then taken for a longer run in hot weather, the accumulated oil will burn off producing ominous smoke from the exhaust.

### 33 Black smoke (caused by over-rich mixture)

● Air filter element clogged. Clean or renew the element.
● Main jet loose or too large. Remove the float chamber to check for tightness of the jet. If the machine is used at high altitudes rejetting will be required to compensate for the lower atmospheric pressure.
● Cold start mechanism jammed on. Check that the mechanism works smoothly and correctly.
● Fuel level too high. The fuel level is controlled by the float height which can increase as a result of wear or damage. Remove the float bowl and check the float height. Check also that floats have not punctured; a punctured float will lose buoyancy and allow an increased fuel level.
● Float valve needle stuck open. Caused by dirt or a worn valve. Clean the float chamber or renew the needle and, if necessary, the valve seat.

## Poor handling or roadholding

### 34 Directional instability

● Steering head bearing adjustment too tight. This will cause rolling or weaving at low speeds. Re-adjust the bearings.
● Steering head bearing worn or damaged. Correct adjustment of the bearing will prove impossible to achieve if wear or damage has occurred. Inconsistent handling will occur including rolling or weaving at low speed and poor directional control at indeterminate higher speeds. The steering head bearing should be dismantled for inspection and renewed if required. Lubrication should also be carried out.
● Bearing races pitted or dented. Impact damage caused, perhaps, by an accident or riding over a pot-hole can cause indentation of the bearing, usually in one position. This should be noted as notchiness when the handlebars are turned. Renew and lubricate the bearings.
● Steering stem bent. This will occur only if the machine is subjected to a high impact such as hitting a curb or a pot-hole. The lower yoke/stem should be renewed; do not attempt to straighten the stem.
● Front or rear tyre pressures too low.
● Front or rear tyre worn. General instability, high speed wobbles and skipping over white lines indicates that tyre renewal may be required. Tyre induced problems, in some machine/tyre combinations, can occur even when the tyre in question is by no means fully worn.
● Swinging arm bearings worn. Difficulties in holding line, particularly when cornering or when changing power settings indicates wear in the swinging arm bearings. The swinging arm should be removed from the machine and the bearings renewed.
● Swinging arm flexing. The symptoms given in the preceding paragraph will also occur if the swinging arm fork flexes badly. This can be caused by structural weakness as a result of corrosion, fatigue or impact damage, or because the rear wheel spindle is slack.
● Wheel bearings worn. Renew the worn bearings.
● Loose wheel spokes. The spokes should be tightened evenly to maintain tension and trueness of the rim.
● Tyres unsuitable for machine. Not all available tyres will suit the characteristics of the frame and suspension, indeed, some tyres or tyre combinations may cause a transformation in the handling characteristics. If handling problems occur immediately after changing to a new tyre type or make, revert to the original tyres to see whether an improvement can be noted. In some instances a change to what are, in fact, suitable tyres may give rise to handling deficiences. In this case a thorough check should be made of all frame and suspension items which affect stability.

### 35 Steering bias to left or right

● Rear wheel out of alignment. Caused by uneven adjustment of chain tensioner adjusters allowing the wheel to be askew in the fork ends. A bent rear wheel spindle will also misalign the wheel in the swinging arm.

● Wheels out of alignment. This can be caused by impact damage to the frame, swinging arm, wheel spindles or front forks. Although occasionally a result of material failure or corrosion it is usually as a result of a crash.

● Front forks twisted in the steering yokes. A light impact, for instance with a pot-hole or low curb, can twist the fork legs in the steering yokes without causing structural damage to the fork legs or the yokes themselves. Re-alignment can be made by loosening the yoke pinch bolts, wheel spindle and mudguard bolts. Re-align the wheel with the handlebars and tighten the bolts working upwards from the wheel spindle. This action should be carried out only when there is no chance that structural damage has occurred.

### 36 Handlebar vibrates or oscillates

● Tyres worn or out of balance. Either condition, particularly in the front tyre, will promote shaking of the fork assembly and thus the handlebars. A sudden onset of shaking can result if a balance weight is displaced during use.

● Tyres badly positioned on the wheel rims. A moulded line on each wall of a tyre is provided to allow visual verification that the tyre is correctly positioned on the rim. A check can be made by rotating the tyre; any misalignment will be immediately obvious.

● Wheels rims warped or damaged. Inspect the wheels for runout as described in Chapter 5.

● Swinging arm bearings worn. Renew the bearings.

● Wheel bearings worn. Renew the bearings.

● Steering head bearings incorrectly adjusted. Vibration is more likely to result from bearings which are too loose rather than too tight. Re-adjust the bearings.

● Loose fork component fasteners. Loose nuts and bolts holding the fork legs, wheel spindle, mudguards or steering stem can promote shaking at the handlebars. Fasteners on running gear such as the forks and suspension should be check tightened occasionally to prevent dangerous looseness of components occurring.

● Engine mounting bolts loose. Tighten all fasteners.

### 37 Poor front fork performance

● Damping fluid level incorrect. If the fluid level is too low poor suspension control will occur resulting in a general impairment of roadholding and early loss of tyre adhesion when cornering and braking. Too much oil is unlikely to change the fork characteristics unless severe overfilling occurs when the fork action will become stiffer and oil seal failure may occur.

● Damping oil viscosity incorrect. The damping action of the fork is directly related to the viscosity of the damping oil. The lighter the oil used, the less will be the damping action imparted. For general use, use the recommended viscosity of oil, changing to a slightly higher or heavier oil only when a change in damping characteristic is required. Overworked oil, or oil contaminated with water which has found its way past the seals, should be renewed to restore the correct damping performance and to prevent bottoming of the forks.

● Damping components worn or corroded. Advanced normal wear of the fork internals is unlikely to occur until a very high mileage has been covered. Continual use of the machine with damaged oil seals which allows the ingress of water, or neglect, will lead to rapid corrosion and wear. Dismantle the forks for inspection and overhaul.

● Weak fork springs. Progressive fatigue of the fork springs, resulting in a reduced spring free length, will occur after extensive use. This condition will promote excessive fork dive under braking, and in its advanced form will reduce the at-rest extended length of the forks and thus the fork geometry. Renewal of the springs as a pair is the only satisfactory course of action.

● Bent stanchions or corroded stanchions. Both conditions will prevent correct telescoping of the fork legs, and in an advanced state can cause sticking of the fork in one position. In a mild form corrosion will cause stiction of the fork thereby increasing the time the suspension takes to react to an uneven road surface. Bent fork stanchions should be attended to immediately because they indicate that impact damage has occurred, and there is a danger that the forks will fail with disastrous consequences.

### 38 Front fork judder when braking (see also Section 50)

● Wear between the fork stanchions and the fork legs. Renewal of the affected components is required.

● Slack steering head bearings. Re-adjust the bearings.

● Warped brake drum. If irregular braking action occurs fork judder can be induced in what are normally serviceable forks. Renew the damaged brake components.

### 39 Poor rear suspension performance

● Rear suspension unit damper worn out or leaking. The damping performance of most rear suspension units falls off with age. This is a gradual process, and thus may not be immediately obvious. Indications of poor damping include hopping of the rear end when cornering or braking, and a general loss of positive stability.

● Weak rear springs. If the suspension unit springs fatigue they will promote excessive pitching of the machine and reduce the ground clearance when cornering. It is probable that if spring fatigue has occurred the damper units will also require renewal.

● Swinging arm flexing or bearings worn. See Sections 34 and 36.

● Bent suspension unit damper rod. This is likely to occur only if the machine is dropped or if seizure of the piston occurs. If either happens the suspension unit should be renewed.

## Abnormal frame and suspension noise

### 40 Front end noise

● Oil level low or too thin. This can cause a 'spurting' sound and is usually accompanied by irregular fork action.

● Spring weak or broken. Makes a clicking or scraping sound. Fork oil will have a lot of metal particles in it.

● Steering head bearings loose or damaged. Clicks when braking. Check, adjust or replace.

● Fork clamps loose. Make sure all fork clamp pinch bolts are tight.

● Fork stanchion bent. Good possibility if machine has been dropped. Repair or replace tube.

### 41 Rear suspension noise

● Fluid level too low. Leakage of a suspension unit, usually evident by oil on the outer surfaces, can cause a spurting noise. The suspension units should be renewed as a pair.

● Defective rear suspension unit with internal damage. Renew the suspension unit.

## Brake problems

### 42 Brakes are spongy or ineffective

● Brake cable deterioration. Damage to the outer cable by stretching or being trapped will give a spongy feel to the brake lever. The cable should be renewed. A cable which has become corroded due to old age or neglect of lubrication will partially seize making operation very heavy. Lubrication at this stage may overcome the problem but the fitting of a new cable is recommended.

● Worn brake linings. Determine lining wear using the external brake wear indicator on the brake backplate, or by removing the wheel and withdrawing the brake backplate. Renew the shoe/lining units as a pair if the linings are worn below the recommended limit.

● Worn brake camshaft. Wear between the camshaft and the bearing surface will reduce brake feel and reduce operating efficiency. Renewal of one or both items will be required to rectify the fault.

● Worn brake cam and shoe ends. Renew the worn components.

● Linings contaminated with dust or grease. Any accumulations of dust should be cleaned from the brake assembly and drum using a petrol dampened cloth. Do not blow or brush off the dust because it is asbestos based and thus harmful if inhaled. Light contamination from grease can be removed from the surface of the brake linings using a solvent; attempts at removing heavier contamination are less likely to be successful because some of the lubricant will have been absorbed by the lining material which will severely reduce the braking performance.

## 43  Brake drag

● Incorrect adjustment. Re-adjust the brake operating mechanism.
● Drum warped or oval. This can result from overheating or impact or uneven tension of the wheel spokes. The condition is difficult to correct, although if slight ovality only occurs, skimming the surface of the brake drum can provide a cure. This is work for a specialist engineer. Renewal of the complete wheel hub is normally the only satisfactory solution.
● Weak brake shoe return springs. This will prevent the brake lining/shoe units from pulling away from the drum surface once the brake is released. The springs should be renewed.
● Brake camshaft, lever pivot or cable poorly lubricated. Failure to attend to regular lubrication of these areas will increase operating resistance which, when compounded, may cause tardy operation and poor release movement.

## 44  Brake lever or pedal pulsates in operation

● Drums warped or oval. This can result from overheating or impact or uneven spoke tension. This condition is difficult to correct, although if slight ovality only occurs skimming the surface of the drum can provide a cure. This is work for a specialist engineer. Renewal of the hub is normally the only satisfactory solution.

## 45  Drum brake noise

● Drum warped or oval. This can cause intermittent rubbing of the brake linings against the drum. See the preceding Section.
● Brake linings glazed. This condition, usually accompanied by heavy lining dust contamination, often induces brake squeal. The surface of the linings may be roughened using glass-paper or a fine file.

## 46  Brake induced fork judder

● Worn front fork stanchions and legs, or worn or badly adjusted steering head bearings. These conditions, combined with uneven or pulsating braking as described in Section 44 will induce more or less judder when the brakes are applied, dependent on the degree of wear and poor brake operation. Attention should be given to both areas of malfunction. See the relevant Sections.

## Electrical problems

## 47  Battery dead or weak

● Battery faulty. Battery life should not be expected to exceed 3 to 4 years, particularly where a starter motor is used regularly. Gradual sulphation of the plates and sediment deposits will reduce the battery performance. Plate and insulator damage can often occur as a result of vibration. Complete power failure, or intermittent failure, may be due to a broken battery terminal. Lack of electrolyte will prevent the battery maintaining charge.
● Battery leads making poor contact. Remove the battery leads and

clean them and the terminals, removing all traces of corrosion and tarnish. Reconnect the leads and apply a coating of petroleum jelly to the terminals.
● Load excessive. If additional items such as spot lamps, are fitted, which increase the total electrical load above the maximum alternator output, the battery will fail to maintain full charge. Reduce the electrical load to suit the electrical capacity.
● Rectifier failure.
● Alternator generating coils open-circuit or shorted.
● Charging circuit shorting or open circuit. This may be caused by frayed or broken wiring, dirty connectors or a faulty ignition switch. The system should be tested in a logical manner. See Section 50.

## 48  Battery overcharged

● Regulator faulty. Overcharging is indicated if the battery becomes hot or it is noticed that the electrolyte level falls repeatedly between checks. In extreme cases the battery will boil causing corrosive gases and electrolyte to be emitted through the vent pipes.
● Battery wrongly matched to the electrical circuit. Ensure that the specified battery is fitted to the machine.

## 49  Total electrical failure

● Fuse blown. Check the main fuse. If a fault has occurred, it must be rectified before a new fuse is fitted.
● Battery faulty. See Section 47.
● Earth failure. Check that the frame main earth strap from the battery is securely affixed to the frame and is making a good contact.
● Ignition switch or power circuit failure. Check for current flow through the battery positive lead (red) to the ignition switch. Check the ignition switch for continuity.

## 50  Circuit failure

● Cable failure. Refer to the machine's wiring diagram and check the circuit for continuity. Open circuits are a result of loose or corroded connections, either at terminals or in-line connectors, or because of broken wires. Occasionally, the core of a wire will break without there being any apparent damage to the outer plastic cover.
● Switch failure. All switches may be checked for continuity in each switch position, after referring to the switch position boxes incorporated in the wiring diagram for the machine. Switch failure may be a result of mechanical breakage, corrosion or water.
● Fuse blown. Refer to the wiring diagram to check whether or not a circuit fuse is fitted. Replace the fuse, if blown, only after the fault has been identified and rectified.

## 51  Bulbs blowing repeatedly

● Vibration failure. This is often an inherent fault related to the natural vibration characteristics of the engine and frame and is, thus, difficult to resolve. Modifications of the lamp mounting, to change the damping characteristics, may help.
● Intermittent earth. Repeated failure of one bulb, particularly where the bulb is fed directly from the generator, indicates that a poor earth exists somewhere in the circuit. Check that a good contact is available at each earthing point in the circuit.
● Reduced voltage. Where a quartz-halogen bulb is fitted the voltage to the bulb should be maintained or early failure of the bulb will occur. Do not overload the system with additional electrical equipment in excess of the system's power capacity and ensure that all circuit connections are maintained clean and tight.

**Castrol Lubricants**

## Castrol Engine Oils
### Castrol Grand Prix

Castrol Grand Prix 10W/40 four stroke motorcycle oil is a superior quality lubricant designed for air or water cooled four stroke motorcycle engines, operating under all conditions.

### Castrol Super TT Two Stroke Oil

Castrol Super TT Two Stroke Oil is a superior quality lubricant specially formulated for high powered Two Stroke engines. It is readily miscible with fuel and contains selective modern additives to provide excellent protection against deposit induced pre-ignition, high temperature ring sticking and scuffing, wear and corrosion.
Castrol Super TT Two Stroke Oil is recommended for use at petrol mixture ratios of up to 50:1.

### Castrol R40

Castrol R40 is a castor-based lubricant specially designed for racing and high speed rallying, providing the ultimate in lubrication. Castrol R40 should never be mixed with mineral-based oils, and further additives are unnecessary and undesirable. A specialist oil for limited applications.

## Castrol Gear Oils
### Castrol Hypoy EP90

An SAE 90 mineral-based extreme pressure multi-purpose gear oil, primarily recommended for the lubrication of conventional hypoid differential units operating under moderate service conditions. Suitable also for some gearbox applications.

### Castrol Hypoy Light EP 80W

A mineral-based extreme pressure multi-purpose gear oil with similar applications to Castrol Hypoy but an SAE rating of 80W and suitable where the average ambient temperatures are between 32°F and 10°F. Also recommended for manual transmissions where manufacturers specify an extreme pressure SAE 80 gear oil.

### Castrol Hypoy B EP80 and B EP90

Are mineral-based extreme pressure multi-purpose gear oils with similar applications to Castrol Hypoy, operating in average ambient temperatures between 90°F and 32°F. The Castrol Hypoy B range provides added protection for gears operating under very stringent service conditions.

## Castrol Greases
### Castrol LM Grease

A multi-purpose high melting point lithium-based grease suitable for most automotive applications, including chassis and wheel bearing lubrication.

### Castrol MS3 Grease

A high melting point lithium-based grease containing molybdenum disulphide. Suitable for heavy duty chassis application and some CV joints where a lithium-based grease is specified.

### Castrol BNS Grease

A bentone-based non melting high temperature grease for ultra severe applications such as race and rally car front wheel bearings.

## Other Castrol Products
### Castrol Girling Universal Brake and Clutch Fluid

A special high performance brake and clutch fluid with an advanced vapour lock performance. It is the only fluid recommended by Girling Limited and surpasses the performance requirements of the current SAE J1703 Specification and the United States Federal Motor Vehicle Safety Standard No. 116 DOT 3 Specification.
In addition, Castrol Girling Universal Brake and Clutch fluid fully meets the requirements of the major vehicle manufacturers.

### Castrol Fork Oil

A specially formulated fluid for the front forks of motorcycles, providing excellent damping and load carrying properties.

### Castrol Chain Lubricant

A specially developed motorcycle chain lubricant containing non-drip, anti corrosion and water resistant additives which afford excellent penetration, lubrication and protection of exposed chains.

### Castrol Everyman Oil

A light-bodied machine oil containing anti-corrosion additives for both household use and cycle lubrication.

### Castrol DWF

A de-watering fluid which displaces moisture, lubricates and protects against corrosion of all metals. Innumerable uses in both car and home. Available in 400gm and 200gm aerosol cans.

### Castrol Easing Fluid

A rust releasing fluid for corroded nuts, locks, hinges and all mechanical joints. Also available in 250ml tins.

### Castrol Antifreeze

Contains anti-corrosion additives with ethylene glycol. Recommended for the cooling system of all petrol and diesel engines.

# YAMAHA DT 50 & 80 TRAIL BIKES

## Check list

**Daily**

1  Check the level of engine oil in the tank

**Weekly or every 150 miles (250 km)**
1  Check the machine for loose fittings and leaks
2  Check the operation of the lights, horn and speedometer
3  Check the tyre pressures
4  Inspect the tyres for wear and damage
5  Lubricate the exposed portions of control cables
6  Lubricate the final drive chain
7  Check the gearbox oil level

**Fortnightly or every 300 miles (500 km)**
1  Adjust the final drive chain
2  Check the battery

**Monthly, or every 900 miles (1500 km)**
1  Check the final drive chain for wear
2  Clean and examine the air filter

**Two monthly or every 1800 miles (3000 km)**
1  Change the gearbox oil
2  Adjust the clutch
3  Adjust the carburettor
4  Adjust the throttle cable
5  Clean the spark plug and check the electrode gap
6  Lubricate the contact breaker cam wick
7  Grease all stand pivots, handlebar levers and footrests
8  Lubricate all control cables
9  Lubricate the speedometer cable
10 Check the steering head bearings for play
11 Examine the wheels and check for wear in the bearings
12 Adjust the brakes and check the degree of wear

**Four monthly or every 3700 miles (6000 km)**
1  Decarbonize the cylinder head, barrrel and exhaust system
2  Adjust and bleed the oil pump
3  Clean the tap fuel filter
4  Examine the fuel feed pipe for splitting and deterioration
5  Renew the spark plug
6  Reset the contact breaker gap and check the timing
7  Renew the front fork oil
8  Grease the steering head bearing
9  Lubricate the swinging arm pivot
10 Examine and lubricate the wheel bearings
11 Lubricate the speedometer drive gear
12 Lubricate the brake cam shaft

## Adjustment data

| Tyre pressures | Front | Rear |
|---|---|---|
| DT50 M | 14 psi (1.0 kg/cm²) | 17 psi (1.2 kg/cm²) |
| All others | 21 psi (1.5 kg/cm²) | 26 psi (1.8 kg/cm²) |

**Spark plug type**
DT80 MX            NGK B8HS
All others          NGK B7HS

**Spark plug gap**       0.6 mm (0.024 in)

**Contact breaker gap**  0.3 – 0.4 mm (0.011   0.015 in)

**Ignition timing**      1.65 – 1.95 mm (0.064   0.076 in) BTDC

**Idle speed**
DT50 MX            1250 rpm
All others          1300 rpm

25 ~ 30 mm

Chain free play measurement

Chain adjustment

**Final drive chain check and adjustment**
1  Split pin
2  Castellated nut
3  Adjusting bolt
4  Alignment marks

## Recommended lubricants

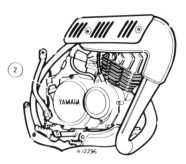

H 12296

| Component | Quantity | Type/viscosity |
|---|---|---|
| 1  Engine | 1.0 lit (1.76 Imp pt) | Good quality non-diluent 2-stroke oil SAE 10W/30 |
| 2  Gearbox   at oil change | | SAE 10W/30 |
| DT50 M | 550 cc (0.97 Imp pt) | |
| All others | 600 cc (1.05 Imp pt) | |
| 3  Front forks | | |
| DT50 M | 140 cc (4.93 Imp fl oz) | SAE 10W/30 motor oil |
| All others | 208 cc (7.32 Imp fl oz) | SAE 10 fork oil |
| 4  Final drive chain | As required | Aerosol chain lubricant |
| 5  Wheel bearings | As required | High melting point grease |
| 6  Steering head bearings | As required | High melting point grease |
| 7  Swinging arm pivot shaft | As required | High melting point grease |
| 8  Pivot points | As required | Lithium base grease |
| 9  Control cables | As required | SAE 10W/30 motor oil |

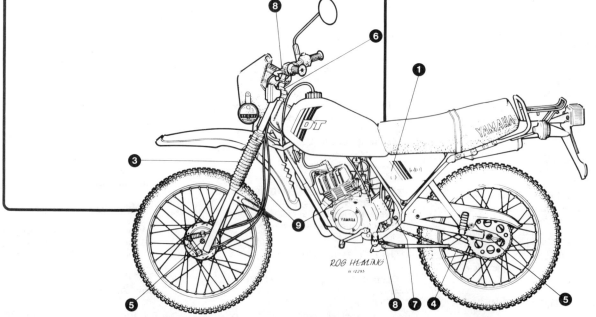

ROG HEALING
H 12295

# ROUTINE MAINTENANCE GUIDE

# Routine maintenance

Periodic routine maintenance is a continuous process which should commence immediately the machine is used. The object is to maintain all adjustments and to diagnose and rectify minor defects before they develop into more extensive, and often more expensive, problems.

It follows that if the machine is maintained properly, it will both run and perform with optimum efficiency, and be less prone to unexpected breakdowns. Regular inspection of the machine will show up any parts which are wearing, and with a little experience, it is possible to obtain the maximum life from any one component, renewing it when it becomes so worn that it is liable to fail.

Regular cleaning can be considered as important as mechanical maintenance. This will ensure that all the cycle parts are inspected regularly and are kept free from accumulations of road dirt and grime.

Cleaning is especially important during the winter months, despite its appearance of being a thankless task which very soon seems pointless. On the contrary, it is during these months that the paintwork, chromium plating, and the alloy casings suffer the ravages of abrasive grit, rain and road salt. A couple of hours spent weekly on cleaning the machine will maintain its appearance and value, and highlight small points, like chipped paint, before they become a serious problem.

The various maintenance tasks are described under their respective mileage and calendar headings, and are accompanied by diagrams and photographs where pertinent.

It should be noted that the intervals between each maintenance task serve only as a guide. As the machine gets older, or if it is used under particularly arduous conditions, it is advisable to reduce the period between each check.

Although no special tools are required for routine maintenance, a good selection of general workshop tools is essential. Included in the tools must be a range of metric ring or combination spanners, a selection of crosshead screwdrivers, and two pairs of circlip pliers, one external opening and the other internal opening. Additionally, owing to the extreme tightness of most casing screws on Japanese machines, an impact screwdriver, together with a choice of large or small crosshead screw bits, is absolutely indispensable. This is particularly so if the engine has not been dismantled since leaving the factory.

## Daily

### 1   Engine oil level check

Although it is safe to use the machine as long as oil is visible in the tank sight glass, it is recommended that the level is maintained to within approximately an inch of the filler hole to allow a good reserve. Detach the left-hand sidepanel to expose the filler cap.

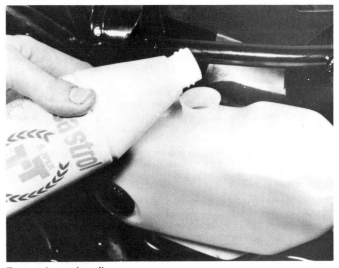

Top up the engine oil

## Weekly, or every 150 miles (250 km)

### 1   Safety check

Give the machine a thorough inspection, checking for loose fasteners, frayed control cables, severe oil and petrol leaks, etc.

### 2   Legal check

Check the lights and horn are working properly and clean the lenses. It is an offence to ride a machine with defective lights, even in daylight. The horn is also a statutory requirement.

### 3   Tyre pressure check

Check pressures with the tyres cold, using an accurate gauge. Purchase a pocket gauge to offset inaccuracies between garage forecourt instruments. Refer to the Routine Maintenance Guide for correct pressures.

### 4   Tyre wear and damage check

Inspect the tyres for splits or cracks which may develop into serious faults. Remove small stones, etc from between the tread blocks. Renew a tyre with a tread depth less than 4 mm (0.16 in).

## 5   Control cable lubrication

Apply a few drops of motor oil to the exposed inner of each cable. This will prevent the cables drying-up before the more thorough 2 monthly lubrication.

## 6   Final drive chain lubrication

With the chain fitted, spray it with one of the proprietary chain greases sold in aerosol form. Engine oil can be used but its effective life is limited due to the speed with which it is flung off the chain.

## 7   Gearbox oil level check

Run the engine for a few minutes. Remove the filler plug adjacent to the kickstart lever. Insert the level gauge and lift the machine off its stand so that it is vertical. Oil level is correct if it is between the maximum and minimum marks on the gauge. Refit the filler plug.

---

**Fortnightly, or every 300 miles (500 km)**

---

Complete the weekly tasks and carry out the following:-

## 1   Final drive chain adjustment

Check chain movement with the machine unloaded and resting on both wheels. Rotate the rear wheel and find the chain tight spot. On DT50 M models, position the tight spot in the centre of the lower chain run; on MX models position it directly beneath the pillion footrest. The correct up and down movement is 20-25 mm (0.8 – 1.0 in) for DT50 M models or 30 mm (1.2 in) for MX models, measured at the tight spot.

Before adjustment, remove the split-pin from the wheel spindle retaining nut and loosen the nut. Loosen the torque arm to brake backplate nut. Tighten the chain by turning each adjuster nut clockwise an equal number of turns. Verify wheel alignment by checking each adjuster mark is aligned with the same mark on each fork end.

Upon completion, tighten the spindle retaining nut to 6.0 kgf m (43.3 lbf ft) torque loading and the torque arm nut to 1.8 kgf m (13.0 lbf ft). Lock the spindle nut with a new split-pin. Tighten each adjuster nut $\frac{1}{4}$ turn. Check the wheel spins freely and if necessary, adjust the rear brake.

An overtight chain will place excessive loads on the gearbox and rear wheel bearings, leading to their early failure. It will also absorb a surprising amount of power.

## 2   Battery electrolyte level check

Check the electrolyte level is between the upper and lower marks on the battery case. If necessary, replenish each cell with distilled water. Do not overfill. Check the vent pipe is attached and correctly routed.

Loosen the torque arm nut ...

... turn each chain adjuster, noting the alignment marks ...

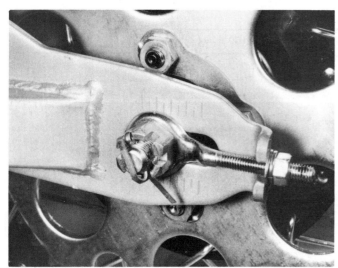

... lock the spindle nut with a new split-pin

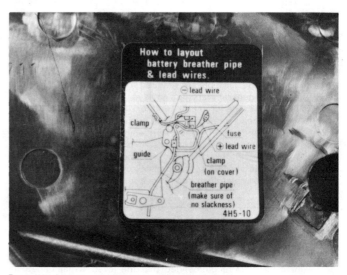

Route the battery vent pipe correctly

## Monthly, or every 900 miles (1500 km)

Complete the preceding tasks and carry out the following.

### 1 Final drive chain wear check and renewal

Pull the chain off the wheel sprocket at the point shown in the accompanying figure. If the chain lifts more than one half tooth depth, renew the chain.

To renew the chain, loosen the wheel spindle nut, torque arm nut and adjuster nuts before pushing the wheel forward. Rotate the wheel so the split link is at the wheel sprocket. Using flat-nose pliers, remove the spring clip from the link and withdraw the link. Join the new and old chains and use the old chain to pull the new one over the gearbox sprocket. Connect the ends of the new chain with the new link provided; the spring clip must have the side plate fitted beneath it, be seated correctly and have its closed end facing the direction of chain travel. Readjust the chain; see the preceding Section.

Replacement chains are available from Renold Limited, the British chain manufacturer. When ordering, quote chain size, the number of links and machine type.

### 2 Air filter element examination and cleaning
**DT50 M**

Detach the left-hand sidepanel. Remove the retaining screw with washer and detach the filter cover. With the element removed, pull it off its guide.

**DT50 MX and 80 MX**

Remove the three right-hand sidepanel retaining screws with washers. Remove the panel, taking care not to tear its seal. Remove the element. Renew the seal if broken or perished.

**All models**

Renew the element if hardened or badly clogged. If serviceable, immerse the element in white spirit, gently squeezing it to remove all oil and dist. Remove excess solvent by pressing the element between the palms of the hands; wringing it out will cause damage. Allow a short time for any remaining solvent to evaporate.

Reimpregnate the element with clean SAE 10W/30 oil and gently squeeze out any excess. On DT50 M models, coat the element sealing edges with light grease.

When fitting, position the element and its cover correctly. Air which bypasses the element will carry dirt into the carburettor and crankcase and will weaken the fuel/air mixture.

If riding in a particularly dusty or moist atmosphere, increase the frequency of cleaning the element. Never run the engine without the element fitted; the carburettor is jetted to compensate for its being fitted and the resulting weak mixture will cause overheating of the engine.

## Two monthly, or every 1800 miles (3000 km)

Complete the preceding tasks and carry out the following.

### 1 Gearbox oil change

Position a container of at least 700 cc (1.2 Imp pint) capacity beneath the engine. Remove the drain plug from the underside of the crankcase. Whilst waiting for the oil to drain, examine the plug sealing washer and renew if damaged.

On completion of draining, refit the plug and tighten it to 2.0 kgf m (14.5 lbf ft). Remove the filler plug adjacent to the kickstart lever and replenish the gearbox with the specified quantity of SAE 10W/30 oil, see Chapter 2. Check the oil level with the gauge and refit the filler plug.

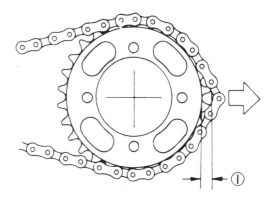

**Checking final drive chain wear**
*1   Maximum wear limit*

Clean the air filter element (MX shown)

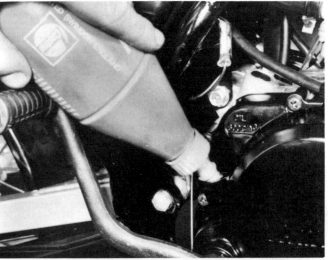

Replenish the gearbox with oil

## 2   Clutch adjustment

Slacken the clutch cable adjusting locknut and screw in the adjuster so that there is plenty of play in the cable.

Remove the outer left-hand crankcase cover. Loosen the adjuster locknut. Turn the adjuster screw slowly clockwise until it seats lightly against the pushrod. Turn the screw anti-clockwise $\frac{1}{4}$ turn and tighten its locknut. Refit the cover.

When correctly adjusted, there should be 2 – 3 mm (0.08 – 0.12 in) of free play in the cable inner, measured between the pivot end of the handlebar lever and its retaining clamp. Obtain this play by rotating the adjuster. Retighten the locknut on completion.

## 3   Carburettor adjustment

Start the engine and let it reach its normal operating temperature. Set the throttle stop screw to give the slowest possible idle speed. Turn the pilot air screw in by a fraction of a turn at a time until the engine begins to falter; now turn it out whilst counting the number of turns required to reach the point where the engine again begins to falter. The correct pilot screw position is mid-way between the two extremes, where the engine is idling at its fastest. This should be close to the specified setting, see Chapter 2. If necessary, turn the throttle stop screw to achieve the specified idle speed.

Guard against the possibility of incorrect adjustment which will result in a weak mixture. Two-stroke engines are very susceptible to this type of fault, causing rapid overheating and often subsequent engine seizure. Changes in carburation leading to a weak mixture will occur if the air cleaner is removed or disconnected, or the exhaust system tampered with.

## 4   Throttle cable adjustment

Adjustment is correct when there is 5 – 7 mm (0.20 – 0.30 in) of free play in the cable inner, measured by rotation of the twistgrip. Obtain this play by loosening the cable adjuster locknut and rotating the adjuster. Retighten the locknut on completion.

## 5   Spark plug check

Check the plug type, see Chapter 3, and replace if incorrect. Clean the electrodes with a small brass-wire brush, removing stubborn carbon deposits by scraping with a pocket knife whilst taking care not to chip the porcelain insulator of the centre electrode. Pass a small fine file or emery paper between the electrode faces and remove all traces of abrasive material from the plug on completion of cleaning.

Some local garages and dealers have plug cleaning machines and will clean plugs for a nominal fee. This is a very efficient method but check there is no blasting medium rammed between the insulator and plug body before fitting.

Reset the electrode gap to 0.6 mm (0.024 in), using a feeler gauge which should be a light sliding fit. Bend the outer electrode to alter the gap; never apply force to the centre electrode.

Lightly smear the plug threads with graphite grease. Check the sealing washer is fitted. Do not overtighten the plug, see torque settings, Chapter 1. Always carry a spare plug.

Before reconnecting the suppressor cap, check its seals and renew if damaged or perished. Check the cap is a good firm fit; it contains the suppressor which eliminates TV and radio interference.

## 6   Contact breaker wick lubrication

Remove the outer left-hand crankcase cover. Rotate the generator rotor so the wick can be seen through one of its slots. Apply one or two drops of light machine oil to the wick, taking care to keep oil off the point contact surfaces. Refit the cover.

## 7   General lubrication

Work around the machine, applying grease or oil to any pivot points. These should include the footrests, prop stand, brake pedal, twistgrip, brake cable trunnions, handlebar levers and kickstart.

## 8   Control cable lubrication

Do not lubricate nylon lined cables which may have been fitted as replacements; this can cause total seizure by swelling the nylon.

Lubricate each cable with motor oil using either a hydraulic oiler, which can be purchased from a dealer, or by using the method indicated in the accompanying figure.

Turn the clutch adjuster screw

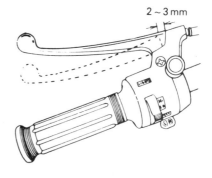

2 ~ 3 mm

Clutch handlebar lever play

Adjust the pilot air screw

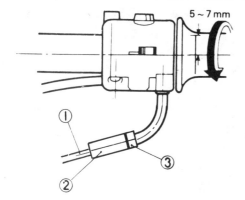

**Throttle cable adjuster**

1  Cable          3  Locknut
2  Adjuster

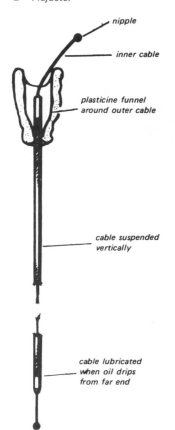

**Oiling a control cable**

## 9   Speedometer cable lubrication

Remove the cable and withdraw its inner. If this is not possible, a badly seized cable will have to be renewed. Wipe the inner with a petrol soaked rag and examine it for broken strands or damage. Do not pull the inner through the hand, broken strands will tear the skin; use a piece of rag.

Lubricate the inner with high melting-point grease. Do not grease the six inches closest to the instrument head; grease will work into the instrument and immobilise the sensitive movement.

## 10   Steering head bearing check and adjustment

Position a stout wooden crate or blocks beneath the engine so that the machine is well supported with the front wheel clear of the ground. Grasp the fork legs near the wheel spindle and push and pull

firmly in a fore and aft direction. If play is evident between the fork yokes and steering head, bearing adjustment is necessary. Play will cause fork judder or imprecise handling.

To adjust, tighten the adjuster ring until resistance is felt then lessen it $\frac{1}{8}$ to $\frac{1}{4}$ turn. It is possible to place a pressure of several tons on the bearings by overtightening, even though the handlebars may turn quite freely. Overtight bearings will cause the machine to roll at low speeds and give imprecise steering. Adjustment is correct if there is no play and the handlebars swing freely to full lock in each direction. A light tap on each end of the handlebars should cause them to swing.

## 11   Wheel examination and bearing check

Raise clear of the ground the wheel to be examined, using blocks positioned beneath the engine. Check the wheel spins freely; if necessary, slacken the brake adjuster and detach the final drive chain.

Examine the rim for serious corrosion or impact damage. Slight deformities can often be corrected by adjusting spoke tension. Serious damage and corrosion will necessitate renewal, which is best left to an expert. A light alloy rim will prove more corrosion resistant.

Place a wire pointer close to the rim and rotate the wheel to check it for runout. If the rim is more than 2.0 mm (0.08 in) out of true in the radial or axial planes, check spoke tension by tapping them with a screwdriver. A loose spoke will sound quite different to those around it. Worn bearings will also cause rim runout.

Adjust spoke tension by turning the square-headed nipples with the appropriate spoke key which can be purchased from a dealer. With the spokes evenly tensioned, remaining distortion can be pulled out by tightening the spokes on one side of the wheel and slackening those directly opposite. This will pull the rim across whilst maintaining spoke tension.

More than slight adjustment will cause the spoke ends to protrude through the nipple and chafe the inner tube, causing a puncture. Remove the tyre and tube and file off the protruding ends. The rim band protects the tube against chafing, check it is in good condition before fitting.

Check spoke tension and general wheel condition regularly. Frequent cleaning will help prevent corrosion. Replace a spoke immediately because the load taken by it will be transferred to adjacent spokes which may fail in turn.

An out of balance wheel will produce a hammering effect through the steering at high speed. Spin the wheel several times. A well balanced wheel will come to rest in any position. One that comes to rest in the same position will have its heaviest part downward and weights must be added to a point diametrically opposite until balance is achieved. Where the tyre has a balance mark on its sidewall (usually a coloured spot), check it is in line with the valve.

Grasp the end of the wheel spindle and spin the wheel. Excessive vibrations felt through the spindle will indicate bearing wear as will a rumble emitted from the wheel centre. Renew the worn bearing(s) as soon as possible, see Chapter 5.

Turn the steering head bearing adjuster ring

## 12 Brake adjustment and wear check

### Front

Adjustment is correct when there is 5 – 8 mm (0.2 – 0.3 in) of free play in the cable inner, measured between the pivot end of the handlebar lever and its retaining clamp. Rotate the cable adjuster at the wheel end to obtain this play. On DT50 M models, retighten the adjuster locknut on completion.

### Rear

Adjustment is correct when there is 25 mm (1.0 in) of movement at the brake pedal footplate. Rotate the adjuster at the wheel end of the brake rod to obtain this movement. Reset the stop lamp switch if necessary, see Chapter 6.

### Both

On completion, check the brake for correct operation. Spin the wheel and apply the brake; there should be no indication of the brake binding. Back off the adjuster until binding disappears and recheck operation.

On MX models, an indicator line on the brake backplate and a pointer on the cam spindle provide an indication of shoe lining wear. The pointer must be inside the arc of the indicator line with the brake fully applied. If not, renew the shoes.

## 13 Final drive chain clean and lubrication

Position a stout wooden crate or blocks beneath the engine so that the machine is well supported with the rear wheel clear of the ground. Lay a length of clean rag beneath the chain. Rotate the wheel to align the chain split link with the wheel sprocket. Using flat-nose pliers, remove the spring clip from the link and withdraw the link.

If an old chain is available, connect it to the one on the machine before it is run off the gearbox sprocket then it can be used to pull the greased chain back over the sprocket. Otherwise, the crankcase cover will have to be renewed.

Wash the chain thoroughly in petrol, observing the necessary fire precautions. Dry the chain and immerse it in a molten lubricant such as Linklyfe or Chainguard. Follow the manufacturer's instructions.

Refit the chain. The spring clip of the link must have the side plate fitted beneath it, be seated correctly and have its closed end facing the direction of chain travel. Check chain adjustment.

## 14 Battery specified gravity check

Remove the battery and check the specific gravity of its acid is 1.260 at 20°C (68°F). Take the reading at the top of the meniscus with the hydrometer vertical.

Protect the eyes and skin against accidental spillage of acid. Eyes contaminated with acid must be immediately flushed with copious amounts of fresh water and examined by a doctor; likewise the skin.

MX models have a brake wear indicator

Fit the chain spring clip correctly

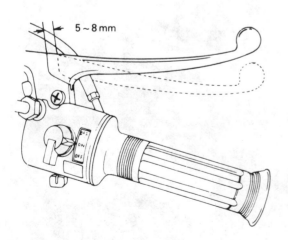
Front brake lever free play

5 ~ 8 mm

---

**Four monthly, or every 3700 miles (6000 km)**

Complete the preceding tasks and carry out the following:

## 1 Decarbonisation

### Cylinder head and barrel

Refer to Chapter 1 and remove the cylinder head and barrel. It is necessary to remove all carbon from the head, barrel and piston crown whilst avoiding removal of the metal surfaces on which it is deposited. Take care when dealing with the soft alloy head and piston. Never use a steel scraper or screwdriver. A hardwood, brass or aluminium scraper is ideal as these are harder than the carbon but no harder than the underlying metal. With the bulk of carbon removed, use a brass wire brush. Finish the head and piston with metal polish; a polished surface will slow the subsequent build-up of carbon. Clean out the barrel ports to prevent the restriction of gas flow. Remove all debris by washing each component in paraffin whilst observing the necessary fire precautions.

### Exhaust system

Remove the exhaust silencer baffle by removing its retaining screw with washer(s), gripping its end with pliers or a mole wrench and pulling it from position. If the baffle has seized in position, pass a tommy bar through the mole wrench and strike it rearwards with a hammer.

Remove and discard any asbestos tape wrapped around the baffle; it need not be replaced. If the build up of carbon and oil on the baffle is not too great, wash it clean with petrol whilst taking the necessary fire precautions. Heavy deposits on the baffle may well indicate similar contamination within the silencer and pipe in which case the system should be removed, see Chapter 2. Clean the baffle by running a blowlamp along its length to burn off the deposits, waiting for it to cool and tapping it sharply with a length of hardwood to dislodge any remaining deposits. Finish with a wire brush and check the baffle holes are clear.

Suspend the two halves of the system, each from its rearmost end. Block the lower end of each half with a cork or wooden bung. Mix up a caustic soda solution (3 lb to over a gallon of fresh water), adding the soda to the water gradually, whilst stirring. Do not pour water into a container of soda, this will cause a violent reaction to take place. Wear proper eye and skin protection; caustic soda is very dangerous. Eyes and skin contaminated by soda must be immediately flushed with fresh water and examined by a doctor. The solution will react violently with aluminium alloy, causing severe damage to any components.

Fill each half of the system with solution, leaving the upper end open. Leave the solution overnight to allow its dissolving action to take place. Ventilate the area to prevent the build-up of noxious fumes. On completion, carefully pour out the solution and flush the system through with clean, fresh water.

Refit the system. On DT50 M models, renew the baffle O-ring. Lightly smear the baffle mating surface and retaining screw threads to prevent seizure. Renew the screw spring washer if flattened.

Do not modify the baffle or run the machine with it removed. This will result in less performance and affect the carburation.

## 2 Oil pump adjustment and bleeding

Remove the pump cover from the right-hand crankcase cover. To check adjustment, rotate the throttle twistgrip slightly to take up any free play in the cable. The pump plunger pin should be aligned with the specified pulley mark, see Chapter 2. If not, loosen the cable adjuster locknut and rotate the adjuster the required amount. Retighten the locknut.

Bleed the pump of air whenever:
a) The machine has fallen on its side
b) The oil tank has run dry
c) Any part of the system has been disconnected

Check the oil tank is full. Hold a piece of clean, absorbent rag beneath the pump and remove the bleed screw. Renew the screw sealing washer, if damaged. Start the engine and allow it to idle. Pull the operating cable fully out of its adjuster to set the pump stroke on maximum. Wait until the oil running from the bleed hole is free of air and refit the screw. Stop the engine and replenish the tank with oil.

The following check need only be done if oil delivery is suspected of being reduced. To check the pump minimum stroke, check cable adjustment and start the engine, allowing it to idle. Observe the adjuster plate carefully and stop the engine directly the plate moves out to its limit. Using a feeler gauge, measure the gap between plate and pulley boss. Repeat the operation and note the largest clearance. The gauge should be a light sliding fit, do not force it into the gap. If the clearance is not as specified in Chapter 2, remove the adjuster plate and change the shim. Renew the spring washer if flattened and refit the plate retaining nut. Recheck the clearance.

## 3 Fuel tap filter clean

Turn the tap lever to 'Off'. Unscrew the collector bowl from the base of the tap body. Remove the filter, having noted its fitted position. Renew the bowl sealing ring, if damaged.

Clean the bowl and filter in clean petrol, using an old toothbrush to remove stubborn contamination. Observe the necessary fire precautions. Examine the filter for splits and holes and renew if defective. Suspect fuel contamination if the filter is clogged; empty and flush the tank. Check the base of the tap is clean. Position the filter correctly and refit the bowl with sealing ring. Nip the bowl tight, turn on the tap and check for leaks. Cure any leaks by reseating the ring and nipping the bowl a little tighter.

Refit the cleaned exhaust baffle (MX shown)

Check pump adjustment ...

... alter pump adjustment by rotating the cable adjuster

Remove the oil pump bleed screw

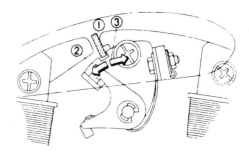

**Adjusting the contact breaker gap**

1   Screwdriver blade      3   Closing direction
2   Opening direction

Check the contact breaker points gap

## 4   Fuel feed pipe examination

Renew the pipe if hard or split. Examine its retaining clips and renew if fatigued. The pipe should be a good firm fit over the fuel tap and carburettor stubs.

## 5   Spark plug renewal

Remove and discard the existing plug, regardless of condition. It will have passed peak efficiency. Fit a new plug of the correct type, see Chapter 3. Before fitting, check the electrode gap is 0.06 mm (0.024 in), smear the plug threads sparingly with graphite grease and check the aluminium crush washer is fitted.

## 6   Contact breaker gap setting and timing check

Remove the outer left-hand crankcase cover. The contact breaker assembly can be viewed through one of the generator rotor slots. Remove the spark plug and turn the rotor until the points begin to open. Use a small screwdriver to push the moving point open against its spring. Examine the point contact faces. If burnt or pitted, refer to Chapter 3 and remove the points for renovation. Light surface deposits can be removed with crocus paper or a piece of stiff card.

With the points in good condition, turn the rotor until they are fully open. Using feeler gauges, check the points gap which should be 0.35 mm (0.14 in). If necessary, alter the gap by loosening the securing screw of the fixed point and moving the point by turning a screwdriver placed in the indentation provided in the edge of its base plate. Retighten the securing screw and recheck the setting.

With the contact breaker gap correctly set, set a multimeter to its resistance function and connect its negative probe to earth on the engine casing. Connect the meter positive (+) probe to the generator ignition source coil lead. Alternatively, use a battery and bulb across the same terminals to provide a test circuit. Use a reasonably high wattage bulb, say 5 watts or more.

Fit a dial test indicator with adaptor into the spark plug hole (Yamaha tool nos 90890 – 03002 and 90890 – 01195). Rotate the crankshaft to bring the piston to top dead centre and zero the DTI scale. Slowly turn the generator rotor clockwise until deflection of the meter needle indicates separation of the breaker points. If a battery and bulb is used the bulb will dim when the points open. Note the DTI reading. Timing is correct if separation occurs 1.80 ± 0.15 mm (0.07 ± 0.006 in) before top dead centre.

It is possible to adjust the breaker gap to achieve separation at this point but the gap and ignition setting must be kept within the specified limits. Wear of the point faces or the fibre heel of the moving point will prevent correct setting in which case renewal of the contact breaker assembly is necessary.

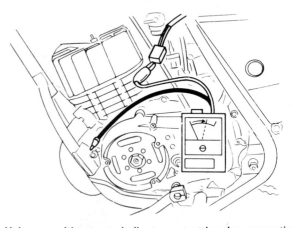

**Using a multimeter to indicate contact breaker separation**

## 7   Fork oil renewal

Remove each fork leg, see Chapter 4. Clamp the stanchion vertically between the protected jaws of a vice. Alternatively, reclamp it in the lower yoke. Remove the top bolt, washer and O-ring. Invert the leg over a suitable container and pump the lower leg up and down the stanchion to assist draining of the oil. Renew the O-ring if flattened or damaged. Replenish with the correct quantity of specified oil, tighten the top bolt and refit the leg.

## 8   Steering head bearing lubrication

The relevant information for carrying out this task is contained in Chapter 4, Section 4.

## 9   Swinging arm pivot lubrication

Position a stout wooden crate or blocks beneath the engine so that the machine is well supported and its weight taken off the rear wheel. Remove the pivot shaft retaining nut (with spring washer – MX models) and use a soft-metal drift and hammer to displace the shaft.

Remove all old lubricant and corrosion from the shaft, using a petrol-soaked rag and emery paper as necessary. Renew the shaft if stepped, badly scored or bent. Renew the spring washer if flattened. Grease the pivot shaft (but not its threads), align the swinging arm in the frame and fit the shaft. Tighten the retaining nut to the specified torque loading.

## 10   Wheel bearing lubrication

With each wheel removed, its bearings can be removed for the purposes of examination and lubrication; see Chapter 5, Section 5.

## 11   Speedometer drive gear lubrication

Refer to Chapter 5 and remove the front wheel. Detach the brake backplate; the drive gear is fitted in its centre. Smear grease around the drive and worm gears.

## 12   Brake cam shaft lubrication

The relevant information for carrying out this task is contained in Chapter 5, Section 10. Failure to lubricate a shaft could well result in its seizing during operation of the brake with disastrous consequences.

### Additional maintenance items

## Cleaning the machine

A machine cleaned regularly will corrode less readily and hence maintain its market value. It will also be more approachable when the time comes for maintenance. Loose or failing components are more easily spotted when not obscured by dirt and oil.

## Metal components

Use a sponge and copious amounts of warm soapy water to wash surface dirt from these components. Remove oil and grease with a solvent such as 'Gunk' or 'Jizer', working it in with a stiff brush when the component is still dry and rinsing it off with fresh water. Keep water out of the carburettor, air filter and electrics.

Except where an aluminium alloy component is lacquered, use a polish such as Solvol Autosol to restore its original lustre. Apply wax polish to the painted components and a good chrome cleaner to those which are chromed. Keep the chain and control cables well lubricated to prevent the ingress of water and wipe the machine down if used in the wet.

## Plastic components

Do not use strong detergents, scouring powders or any abrasive cleaning these components; anything but a mild solution of soapy water may well bleach or score the surface. On completion of cleaning, wipe the component dry with a chamois leather. If the surface finish has faded, use a fine aerosol polish to restore its shine.

# Chapter 1  Engine, clutch and gearbox

## Contents

## Specifications

| | DT50 M and MX | DT80 MX |
|---|---|---|
| **Engine** | | |
| Type ............................................................................ | Air cooled, single cylinder, two-stroke | |
| Bore ............................................................................ | 40.0 mm (1.575 in) | 49.0 mm (1.929 in) |
| Stroke .......................................................................... | 39.7 mm (1.563 in) | 42.0 mm (1.653 in) |
| Capacity ....................................................................... | 49 cc (2.99 cu in) | 79 cc (4.82 cu in) |
| Compression ratio ........................................................... | 5.7 : 1 (M) | 6.4 : 1 (UK) |
| | 6.6 : 1 (MX) | 6.9 : 1 (US) |
| **Cylinder barrel** | | |
| Standard bore ............................................................... | 40.0 – 40.02 mm | 49.0 – 49.02 mm |
| | (1.5748 – 1.5756 in) | (1.921 – 1.9299 in) |
| Taper limit .................................................................... | 0.05 mm (0.002 in) | 0.05 mm (0.002 in) |
| Out of round limit .......................................................... | 0.01 mm (0.0004 in) | 0.01 mm (0.0004 in) |
| **Cylinder head** | | |
| Distortion limit .............................................................. | 0.03 mm (0.0012 in) | 0.03 mm (0.0012 in) |
| Gasket thickness ............................................................ | 0.5 mm (0.02 in) | 0.5 mm (0.02 in) |

## Piston

| | | |
|---|---|---|
| Outside diameter | 40.0 mm (1.575 in) | 49.0 mm (1.929 in) |
| Piston to bore clearance | 0.035 – 0.040 mm (0.0014 – 0.0016 in) | 0.035 – 0.040 mm (0.0014 – 0.0016 in) |
| Oversizes | 40.25, 40.50, 40.75 and 41.0 mm (1.585, 1.594 1.604 and 1.614 in) | 49.25, 49.50, 49.75 and 50.0 mm (1.939, 1.949, 1.959 and 1.969 in) |

## Piston rings

| | | |
|---|---|---|
| Type: | | |
| Top | Keystone | Keystone |
| Second | Keystone | Plain (with expander) |
| Ring to groove clearance: | | |
| Top | 0.02 – 0.06 mm (0.0008 – 0.0024 in) | 0.02 – 0.06 mm (0.0008 – 0.0024 in) |
| Second | 0.02 – 0.06 mm (0.0008 – 0.0024 in) | 0.03 – 0.07 mm (0.0012 – 0.0027 in) |
| End gap (fitted): | | |
| Top and second | 0.15 – 0.35 mm (0.006 – 0.014 in) | 0.15 – 0.35 mm (0.006 – 0.014 in) |

## Crankshaft assembly

| | DT50 M | DT50 MX and 80 MX |
|---|---|---|
| Maximum runout | 0.03 mm (0.0012 in) | 0.03 mm 0.0012 in) |
| Total web width | 38.0 mm (1.496 in) | 37.90 – 37.95 mm (1.492 – 1.494 in) |
| Maximum big-end side clearance | 0.45 mm (0.018 in) | 0.70 mm (0.027 in) |
| Maximum connecting rod deflection | 2.0 (0.08 in) | 2.0 mm (0.08 in) |

## Clutch

| | | |
|---|---|---|
| Type | Wet, multiplate | Wet, multiplate |
| Spring: | | |
| Free length | 31.5 mm (1.240 in) | N/Av |
| Service limit | 30.5 mm (1.201 in) | 34.0 mm (1.338 in) |
| Friction plate: | | |
| Thickness | 3.5 mm (0.14 in) | 3.5 mm (0.14 in) |
| Service limit | 3.2 mm (0.13 in) | 2.7 mm (0.106 in) |
| Plain plate: | | |
| Thickness | 1.6 mm (0.063 in) | 1.6 mm (0.063 in) |
| Maximum warpage | 0.05 mm (0.002 in) | 0.05 mm (0.002 in) |
| Drain axial plug | 0.1 – 0.3 mm (0.004 – 0.012 in) | N/Av |
| Push rod bend limit | 0.15 mm (0.006 in) | 0.15 mm (0.006 in) |

## Gearbox

| | All models | |
|---|---|---|
| Type | 5-speed, constant mesh | |
| Gear ratios (no of teeth): | | |
| 1st | 3.250 : 1 (39/12) | |
| 2nd | 2.000 : 1 (34/17) | |
| 3rd | 1.429 : 1 (30/21) | |
| 4th | 1.125 : 1 (27/24) | |
| 5th | 0.962 : 1 (25/26) | |
| Primary reduction ratio | 3.579 : 1 (68/19) | |
| Secondary reduction ratio: | | |
| DT50 M | 4.182 : 1 (46/11) | |
| DT50 MX | 4.364 : 1 (48/11) | |
| DT80 MX | 2.733 : 1 (41/15) | |

## Torque wrench settings – kgf m (lbf ft)

| | DT50 M | DT50 MX and 80 MX |
|---|---|---|
| Cylinder head retaining nuts | 1.0 (7.2) | 1.5 (10.8) |
| Spark plug | 2.0 (14.5) | 2.5 (18.0) |
| Clutch hub retaining nut | 6.0 (43.3) | 4.5 (32.5) |
| Primary drive pinion retaining nut | 7.0 (51.0) | 6.0 (43.3) |
| Clutch spring retaining bolts | 0.7 (5.0) | 0.6 (4.3) |
| Flywheel generator rotor retaining nut | 5.5 (40.0) | 5.0 (36.1) |
| Gearbox sprocket retaining nut | 6.0 (43.3) | N/App |
| Kickstart lever retaining bolt | 2.0 (14.5) | 1.2 (8.6) |
| | **All models** | |
| Gearchange lever retaining bolt | 1.0 (7.2) | |
| Gearbox oil drain plug | 2.0 (14.5) | |
| Reed valve retaining screws | 0.1 (0.7) | |
| Engine mounting bolts and nuts: | | |
| Front upper | 2.5 (18.0) | |
| Rear upper | 2.5 (18.0) | |
| Rear lower | 3.5 (25.3) | |

## 1   General description

Yamaha DT50 and 80 trail bikes are fitted with a basic single-cylinder, air-cooled, 2-stroke engine of familiar design amongst small Japanese motorcycles.

The engine unit employs vertically split crankcase which house both the crankshaft assembly and the gear clusters. The built-up crankshaft has full flywheels and runs on two journal ball bearings which are housed in the crankcase, the each side of the flywheels. Both small-end and big-end bearings are of the caged needle roller type.

The induction system is of the piston port and reed valve design; where the induction of fuel/air mixture into the crankcase is timed by the reciprocating piston skirt and where an even flow of this mixture is maintained by the reed valve. This valve also serves to reduce the possibility of any blow-back of the combustible gases.

Engine lubrication is by means of the Yamaha Autolube system, in which a gear-driven oil pump draws oil from a separate frame-mounted oil tank and distributes it to the various working parts of the engine. The pump is interconnected to the throttle so that optimum lubrication is achieved at all times, thereby corresponding to the requirements of both engine speed and throttle opening. Lubrication for the gearbox and primary transmission is provided by an oil reservoir shared between the two interconnected assemblies.

A flywheel generator is mounted on the left-hand end of the crankshaft and is fully enclosed behind a detachable crankcase side cover. The clutch is mounted on the right-hand end of the gearbox input shaft and is also fully enclosed. Engine starting is by kickstart; drive being passed from the kickstart shaft pinion to the crankshaft via an idler pinion to the clutch drum and then from the clutch drum onto the crankshaft-mounted primary drive pinion.

## 2   Operations with the engine/gearbox unit in the frame

1   It is not necessary to remove the engine/gearbox unit from the frame in order to carry out the following service operations:

   a)   Removal and fitting of the cylinder head
   b)   Removal and fitting of the cylinder barrel
   c)   Removal and fitting of the piston assembly
   d)   Removal and fitting of the carburettor assembly
   e)   Removal and fitting of the reed valve
   f)   Removal and fitting of the oil pump unit
   g)   Removal and fitting of the clutch assembly and primary drive pinion
   h)   Removal and fitting of the gearchange shaft and pawl or pin mechanism
   i)   Removal and fitting of the kickstart assembly
   j)   Removal and fitting of the flywheel generator and contact breaker assembly
   k)   Removal and fitting of the gearbox sprocket
   l)   Removal and fitting of the neutral indicator switch

## 3   Operations with the engine/gearbox unit removed from the frame

1   Certain operations can be accomplished only if the complete engine unit is removed from the frame. This is because it is necessary to separate the crankcase to gain access to the parts concerned. These operations include:

   a)   Removal and fitting of the crankshaft assembly
   b)   Removal and fitting of the main bearings
   c)   Removal and fitting of the gearbox shaft and pinion assemblies, the gearbox bearings and the gear selector components

## 4   Removing the engine/gearbox unit from the frame

1   Raise the machine to an acceptable working height using a purpose built lift or by building a strong platform. Prevent the machine from rolling forward off its stand by locking on the front brake. To do this, wrap a large rubber band around the lever and twistgrip.

2   Place a container of at least 700 cc (1.2 pint) capacity beneath the engine and remove the gearbox oil drain plug from the underside of the crankcase.

3   Detach each sidepanel and remove the seat. Observe the necessary fire precautions and remove the fuel tank by turning the tap lever to 'Off' unclipping the fuel feed pipe and removing the tank retaining bolt or rubber. On MX models, release the filler cap breather pipe. Pull the tank rearwards off its mounting rubbers and place it in safe storage away from any source of naked flame or sparks. Renew any damaged mounting rubbers.

4   Isolate the battery from the electrical system by disconnecting one of its leads. Doing this will prevent shorting of exposed contacts. It is advisable to service the battery at this stage, see Chapter 6.

5   Unclip the oil feed pipe from the oil tank and drain its contents into a clean container of at least 1.0 litre capacity. On completion, seal the container.

6   Remove the exhaust silencer by detaching it from the frame and exhaust pipe. Release the pipe to cylinder barrel retaining ring and unbolt the pipe from the frame (MX only). Ease the exhaust pipe clear of the frame. Renew any flattened spring washers or damaged seals.

7   Remove the oil pump cover from the right-hand crankcase cover; if necessary, free its retaining screws with an impact driver. Pull the cable retaining clip from the pump pulley, detach the cable from the pulley and pull it clear of the engine.

8   Unscrew the top of the mixing chamber from the carburettor and pull the throttle valve assembly clear of the engine. Wrap this assembly in polythene to prevent contamination. Detach the inlet hose from the carburettor by releasing its clamp. Renew the hose if it is split or perished.

9   Pull the suppressor cap from the spark plug and loosen the plug. Note the fitted position of the gearchange lever and remove the lever. Remove the outer end and inner covers from the left-hand crankcase, using an impact driver if necessary. Free the clutch cable from the inner cover by pulling it clear of the handlebar lever bracket, detaching it from the trunnion of the operating mechanism and pulling it clear of the cover.

10   Trace the leads from the flywheel generator and disconnect them at the nearest push connector. Unclip these leads from the frame.

11   On MX models, remove the gearbox sprocket retaining circlip. Otherwise, remove the sprocket retaining nut after having knocked back its lock washer. It will be necessary to lock the gearbox output shaft by placing the machine in gear and applying the rear brake. Pull the sprocket and chain clear of the engine; if necessary, slacken the chain before doing so.

12   Where a sump guard is fitted, remove its retaining bolts and pull it clear of its mounting rubbers. Remove the engine mounting bolt retaining nuts. On MX models remove the lower mounting bolt. Support the engine, pull out the mounting bolts and ease the engine clear of the machine from the right-hand side.

## 5   Dismantling the engine/gearbox unit: preliminaries

1   Clean the unit by using paraffin and a paintbrush or toothbrush. Do not contaminate electrical components, and mask off points where the paraffin can enter the engine internals. Do not use petrol because of the fire risk.

2   Position the dried unit on a clean work surface. Gather some clean rag, a pen and paper and some small containers suitable for storing engine parts.

3   Before commencing work, carefully read the appropriate procedure. Great force is seldom required to remove a component, if in doubt re-check the procedure.

4   An impact driver is essential for screw removal although it may be possible to replace this with a crosshead screwdriver fitted with a T-handle. Any damaged screws should be renewed or replaced with Allen-headed screws.

## 6   Dismantling the engine/gearbox unit: removing the cylinder head, barrel and piston

1   Remove and examine the spark plug, see Routine Maintenance. Avoid distortion of the cylinder head by slackening its retaining nuts

evenly and in a diagonal sequence. Remove the nuts and washers. Lightly tap the head around its base with a soft-faced hammer to free it and then remove the head. Do not lever the head from position.

2    Release the carburettor from the inlet stub, noting the fitted position of the gasket(s). Disconnect the oil feed pipe from the inlet stub and mask the pipe end.

3    Lightly tap the supported areas of barrel finning around its base to free it from the crankcase. Ease the barrel clear of the crankcase mouth. If the crankcase halves are not to be separated, pack the mouth with clean rag to prevent broken piston rings from falling into the crankcase. Remove the barrel from the engine, taking care to support the piston as it leaves the bore.

4    Remove one of the gudgeon pin circlips. Press the pin free of the piston, remove the piston and the small-end bearing. Discard both circlips.

5    If the gudgeon pin is tight, it will be necessary to warm the piston

to free it. A rag soaked in hot water and wrapped around the piston should suffice. Do not tap the pin from position with the connecting rod unsupported, because bending of the rod may result.

### 7    Dismantling the engine/gearbox unit: removing the oil pump and right-hand crankcase cover

1    Remove the pump retaining screws and ease it far enough out of its housing to allow the oil feed and delivery pipes to be detached. Do not pull these clear of the cover unless they are to be renewed. Upon removal, protect the pump against ingress of dirt.

2    Remove the kickstart lever, having noted its fitted position. Making a template of the cover will provide a reference to the fitted position of its retaining screws. Remove these screws evenly and in a diagonal sequence and pull the cover free of its locating dowels.

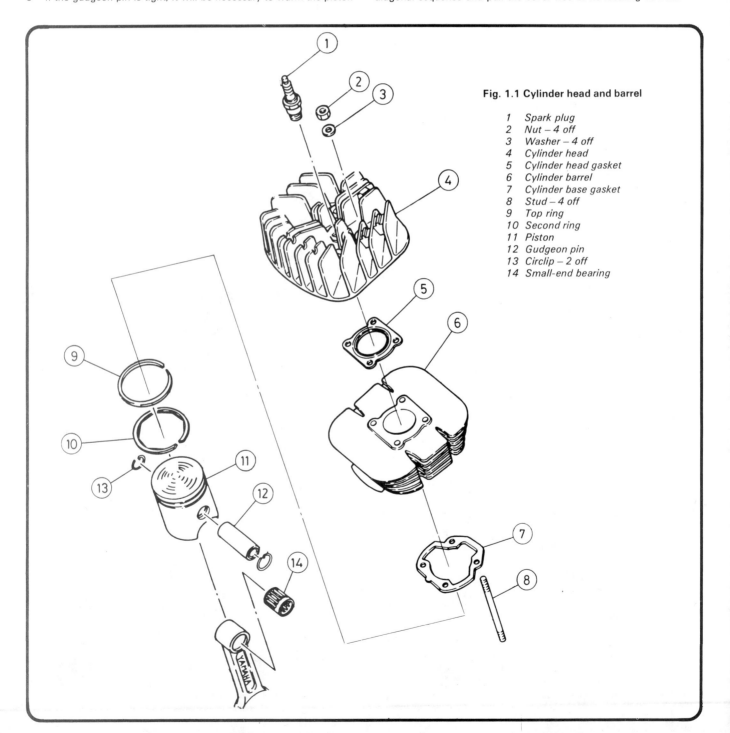

**Fig. 1.1 Cylinder head and barrel**

1    Spark plug
2    Nut – 4 off
3    Washer – 4 off
4    Cylinder head
5    Cylinder head gasket
6    Cylinder barrel
7    Cylinder base gasket
8    Stud – 4 off
9    Top ring
10   Second ring
11   Piston
12   Gudgeon pin
13   Circlip – 2 off
14   Small-end bearing

### 8 Dismantling the engine/gearbox unit: removing the clutch and primary drive pinion

1   Avoid distortion of the clutch pressure plate by slackening its retaining bolts evenly and in a diagonal sequence. Remove the bolts, washers and springs, the pressure plate, the friction and plain plates and the cushion rings (where fitted). Withdraw the two lengths of pushrod and the ball bearing from the gearbox input shaft.

2   Refer to the accompanying photograph and form a tool from a length of metal strip. Lock the clutch hub as shown and remove its retaining nut. Remove the lock washer, the hub, thrust washer, clutch drum with centre bush and the second thrust washer.

3   Lock the crankshaft by passing a close-fitting bar through the small-end eye. Place wooden blocks between the crankcase mouth and bar. Remove the drive pinion retaining nut, its lock washer, the pinion and Woodruff key and the spacer collar.

### 9 Dismantling the engine/gearbox unit: removing the kickstart and gearchange assemblies

1   Using a stout pair of pliers, unhook the kickstart return spring from its stop and restrain it as it unwinds. Pull the kickstart assembly free of the crankcase.

2   Remove the kickstart idler pinion circlip, the plate washer and the pinion. On DT50 M models, remove the wave washer and plain washer.

3   Remove the gearchange selector arm by removing its circlip, releasing its actuating arm from the gearchange drum and pulling it off its pivot. Remove the stepped spacer from the shaft arm, remove the shaft retaining circlip and plate washer and pull the shaft from position.

### 10 Dismantling the engine/gearbox unit: removing the flywheel generator

1   Lock the crankshaft by pressing a close-fitting bar through the small-end eye. Place wooden blocks between the crankcase mouth and bar. Remove the rotor retaining nut, spring washer and plate washer.

2   Use a two-legged puller to remove the rotor from the crankshaft

taper. Position the puller legs as shown in the accompanying photograph. Remove the Woodruff key.

3   Disconnect the electrical lead from the neutral indicator switch. Unclip the stator leads from the crankcase and note the fitted position of the stator. Remove the stator retaining screws and remove the stator.

### 11 Dismantling the engine/gearbox unit: separating the crankcase halves

1   Support the crankcase on the work surface, screw heads uppermost. Make a template to provide a reference to the fitted position of each screw. Remove the screws evenly whilst working in a diagonal sequence.

2   Using a soft-faced hammer, tap around the crankcase joint to break the seal. The crankcase halves can now be tapped apart so that the right-hand half containing the gearbox shafts remains nearest to the work surface. Do not attempt to lever the halves apart. If unsuccessful, obtain Yamaha tool No 90890 – 01135.

8.2 Make a clutch locking tool

8.3 Lock the crankshaft in position

10.2 Pull the rotor off the crankshaft

## 12 Dismantling the engine/gearbox unit: removing the gearbox components and crankshaft

1  Unscrew the detent plunger from the left-hand crankcase half. Move to the right-hand half and remove the circlip from the end of the output shaft. Using an impact driver, release the stop plate securing screws and remove the plate from the drum. Note the fitted position of the selector forks and remove the gearbox components as one unit.
2  Properly support the crankcase half with the crankshaft on wooden blocks so that the crankshaft end is clear of the work surface. Protect the threaded end of the shaft by refitting the appropriate nut, place a heavy copper drift against the shaft and strike it with a heavy hammer to drift the shaft down and clear of the crankcase. Do not use excessive force, if unsuccessful obtain Yamaha tool No 90890 – 01135.

## 13 Examination and renovation: general

1  Before examination, clean each engine part thoroughly in a petrol/paraffin mix whilst observing the necessary fire precautions.
2  Examine each casting for cracks or damage. A crack will require specialist repair. Check each part for wear against the figures given in Specifications. If in doubt, play safe and renew.
3  Repair stripped or badly worn threads by using a thread insert. Refer to your dealer for this service.
4  A screw extractor should be used to remove sheared studs or screws. If unsuccessful or in doubt, consult a professional engineering firm.

## 14 Examination and renewal: crankcase and gearbox oil seals

1  When the crankcase oil seals on a two-stroke engine become worn they admit air into the crankcase and this weakens the incoming fuel/air mixture thereby causing uneven running and difficulty in starting.
2  Carefully examine each seal, especially its lip. Any damage or hardening of a seal will necessitate its immediate renewal. It is advisable to renew the seals as a set, as a matter of course, whilst the engine is dismantled.
3  Remove each seal by prising it from position with the flat of a screwdriver. Avoid damaging the alloy of the seal housing during removal and fitting. A new seal must face in the right direction and enter its housing squarely. Push it in as far as possible by hand and then use a socket and hammer to tap it fully home whilst supporting the casing around the seal housing.

## 15 Examination and renovation: crankcase main bearings and gearbox bearings

1  Vibration felt through the footrests and an audible rumble from the bottom end of the engine will signify failure of the crankshaft main bearings. Wash all oil from the bearings and check for play or roughness. Failure will be obvious.
2  Remove an unserviceable bearing by removing its oil seal or retaining plate, and applying heat to the engine casting. Heat will cause the alloy casing to expand and free the bearing. The safest way to apply heat is to place the casting in an oven set at 80-100°C or to immerse it in boiling water. Do not use excessive or localised heat or warpage may occur. Support the casting and use a hammer and socket to tap the bearing free whilst keeping it square to its housing.
3  Before fitting a new bearing, clean its housing and any oil feed drilling. Reheat and support the casting. Use against the bearing outer race to drift the bearing home.
4  Any bearing fitted in a blind housing will require the use of a slide hammer to remove it. Treat plain bushes in the same manner as roller bearings.

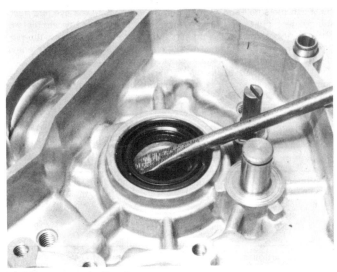

14.3 Remove each oil seal

15.2 Remove defective bearings

## 16 Examination and renovation: crankshaft assembly

1  Big-end failure is characterised by a pronounced knock which will be most noticeable when the engine is worked hard. The usual causes of failure are normal wear, or a failure of the lubrication supply. In the case of the latter, big-end wear will become apparent very suddenly, and will rapidly worsen.
2  Check for wear with the crankshaft set in the TDC (top dead centre) position, by pushing and pulling the connecting rod. No discernible movement will be evident in an unworn bearing, but care must be taken not to confuse end float, which is normal, and bearing wear.
3  If a dial gauge is available, set its pointer against the end of the small-end eye. Measure the side-to-side deflection of the connecting rod. Renew the big-end bearing if the measurement exceeds 2.0 mm (0.08 in).
4  Push the connecting rod to one side and use a feeler gauge to measure the big-end side clearance. Renew the big-end bearing, the crank pin and its washers and the connecting rod if the clearance exceeds that specified.
5  Set the crankshaft on V-blocks positioned on a completely flat surface and measure the amount of deflection with the dial gauge pointer set against the inboard end of the left-hand mainshaft. Renew the crankshaft if the measurement exceeds 0.03 mm (0.0012 in).

6   Push the small-end bearing into the connecting rod eye and push the gudgeon pin through the bearing. Hold the rod steady and feel for movement between it and the pin. If movement is felt, renew the pin, bearing or connecting rod as necessary so no movement exists. Renew the bearing if its roller cage is cracked or worn.

7   Do not attempt to dismantle the crankshaft assembly, this is a specialist task. If a fault is found, return the assembly to a Yamaha agent who will supply a new or service-exchange item.

## 17  Examination and renovation: decarbonising

1   Refer to Routine Maintenance for details of decarbonising the engine and exhaust system.

## 18  Examination and renovation: cylinder head

1   Check that the cylinder head fins are not clogged with oil or road dirt, otherwise the engine will overheat. If necessary, use a degreasing agent and brush to clean between the fins. Check that no cracks are evident, especially in the vicinity of the spark plug or stud holes.

2   Check the condition of the thread in the spark plug hole. If it is damaged an effective repair can be made using a Helicoil thread insert. This service is available from most Yamaha agents. Always use the correct plug and do not overtighten, see Routine Maintenance.

3   Leakage between the head and barrel will indicate distortion. Check the head by placing a straight-edge across several places on its mating surface and attempting to insert a 0.03 mm (0.0012 in) feeler gauge between the two.

4   Remove excessive distortion by rubbing the head mating surface in a slow circular motion against emery paper placed on plate glass. Start with 200 grade paper and finish with 400 grade and oil. Do not remove an excessive amount of metal. If in doubt consult a Yamaha agent.

5   Note that most cases of cylinder head distortion can be traced to unequal tensioning of the cylinder head securing nuts or to tightening them in the incorrect sequence.

## 19  Examination and renovation: cylinder head

1   The usual indication of a badly worn cylinder barrel and piston is piston slap, a metallic rattle that occurs when there is little or no load on the engine.

2   Clean all dirt from between the cooling fins. Carefully remove the ring of carbon from the bore mouth so that bore wear can be accurately assessed.

3   Examine the bore for scoring or other damage, particularly if broken rings are found. Damage will necessitate reboring and a new piston. A satisfactory seal cannot be obtained if the bore is not perfectly finished.

4   There will probably be a lip at the uppermost end of the cylinder bore which marks the limit of travel of the top of the piston ring. The depth of the lip will give some indication of the amount of bore wear that has taken place even though the amount of wear is not evenly distributed.

5   The most accurate method of measuring bore wear is by the use of a cylinder bore DTI (Dial Test Indicator) or a bore micrometer. Measure at the top, middle and bottom of the bore, in-line with the gudgeon pin axis and at 90° to it. Take six measurements in all. Refer to Specifications for standard bore diameter.

6   Alternatively, insert the piston without rings so that it is just below the ridge at the top of the bore. Using a feeler gauge, measure between the bore and the piston side. Repeat the measurement with the piston at the bottom of the bore. Subtract the lesser measurement from the greater. If the difference exceeds 0.02 mm (0.001 in) then suspect excessive wear.

7   Note the figures given in Specifications for taper limit and out of round limit. If a rebore is necessary, note the piston oversizes.

8   After a rebore, the edges of each port should be chamfered to prevent the piston rings catching on them and breaking. This requires careful use of a scraper with fine emery paper to finish. Take care not to damage the bore.

9   Measure piston to bore clearance either by direct measurement of the piston and bore diameter and subtraction or by measurement of the gap with a feeler gauge. Piston diameter must be measured 5 mm (0.20 in) from the base of its skirt and at right-angles to the gudgeon pin hole. If the clearance measured exceeds that given in Specifications, a new piston or rebore and new piston is required.

10  Refer to the preceding Section and check the barrel to head mating surface for distortion.

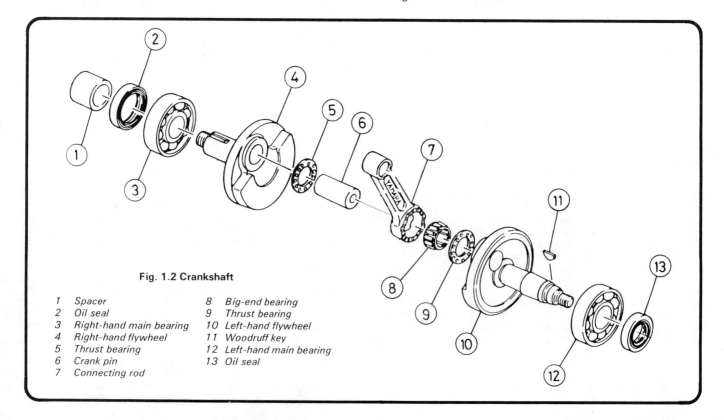

**Fig. 1.2 Crankshaft**

| | | | |
|---|---|---|---|
| 1 | Spacer | 8 | Big-end bearing |
| 2 | Oil seal | 9 | Thrust bearing |
| 3 | Right-hand main bearing | 10 | Left-hand flywheel |
| 4 | Right-hand flywheel | 11 | Woodruff key |
| 5 | Thrust bearing | 12 | Left-hand main bearing |
| 6 | Crank pin | 13 | Oil seal |
| 7 | Connecting rod | | |

### 20 Examination and renovation: piston and piston rings

1   Disregard the existing piston and rings if a rebore is necessary; they will be replaced with oversize items.

2   The rings are brittle and will break easily if overstressed. Pull the ring ends apart with the thumbs and ease the ring from its groove. Refer to the accompanying figure and use strips of tin to ease free a ring which is gummed in its groove. Note the fitted position of each ring.

3   Piston wear usually occurs at its skirt, taking the form of vertical streaks or scoring on the thrust side. There may be some variation in skirt thickness.

4   Measure piston diameter 5 mm (0.20 in) from the base of its skirt, at right-angles to the gudgeon pin hole. If the measurement is less than that specified, renew the piston.

5   Slight scoring of the piston can be removed by careful use of a fine swiss file. Use chalk to prevent clogging of the file teeth and the subsequent risk of scoring. Bad scoring will indicate the need for piston renewal.

6   Any build-up of carbon in the ring grooves can be removed by using a section of broken piston ring, the end of which has been ground to a chisel edge. Using a feeler gauge, measure each ring to groove clearance. Renew the piston if the measurement obtained exceeds that given in Specifications.

7   If the ring locating pegs are loose or worn, renew the piston.

8   The gudgeon pin should be a firm press fit in the piston. Check for scoring on the bearing surfaces of each part and where damage or wear is found, renew the part affected. The pin circlip retaining grooves must be undamaged; renew the piston rather than risk damage to the bore through a circlip becoming detached.

9   Discoloured areas on the working surface of each piston ring indicate the blow-by of gas and the need for renewal.

10   Measure ring wear by inserting each ring into part of the bore which is unworn and measuring the gap between the ring ends with a feeler gauge. If the measurement exceeds that given in Specifications, renew the ring. Use the piston crown to locate the ring squarely in the bore.

11   Remove the wear ridge at the top of the bore before fitting new rings otherwise the top ring will strike the ridge and break. This should be included in the 'glaze busting' process carried out to break down surface glaze on the used bore so that new rings can bed in. Refer to the Yamaha agent for this service.

12   Refit each ring correctly in its previously noted position, checking that it presses easily into its groove and that its ends locate correctly over the peg. As with part worn rings, the end gap of new rings must be measured. If necessary, carefully use a needle file to enlarge the gap.

20.12 Locate the ring ends over the peg

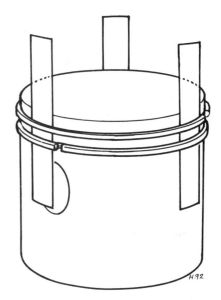

Fig. 1.3 Removing gummed piston rings

20.6 Measure the piston ring to groove clearance

### 21 Examination and renovation: gearbox components

1   Examine each gear pinion for chipped or broken teeth or rounded dogs and renew each damaged item. When dismantling and re-assembling each shaft assembly, refer to the accompanying figure. Gear selection problems will occur if the pinions, washers or circlips are incorrectly fitted. To reduce confusion, reassemble as soon as possible and make rough sketches where necessary. Refer to Section 27.

2   Renew worn or distorted thrust washers and circlips.

3   The 5th gear pinion of the input shaft is a very tight press-fit and should be removed using a hydraulic puller or flypress. This is really a job for the Yamaha agent but if a puller is available, proceed as follows.

4   It is important to appreciate the dangers of using this tool. Set the tool and shaft so that neither can slip. Follow the maker's instructions when assembling the tool; the forces involved are considerable. Protect the eyes against a flawed component suddenly shattering. Before removing the pinion, note its fitted position by measuring with a feeler gauge the gap between it and the 2nd gear pinion.

5   With the gearbox shafts dismantled, inspect the shaft and pinion splines for wear and hairline cracks, renewing each component as necessary. If a pinion has a bushed centre and the bush is overworn,

do not immediately reject the pinion but ask a competent engineer if the bush can be renewed.

6    Clean the gearbox sprocket thoroughly and examine it for hooked or broken teeth and wear of the centre spline. Do not renew the sprocket on its own but renew both sprockets and the chain to prevent rapid wear resulting from the running together of old and new parts.

7    Check for scoring on the bearing surface of the selector fork ends, bores or drum locating pins. Check for cracks around the bore edges and at the base of the fork arms. Where excessive wear of the fork ends and pinion groove is suspected, compare with new items. Renew if in doubt.

8    Place the selector fork shaft on a sheet of plate glass and check for straightness by attempting to insert a feeler gauge beneath it. A bent shaft will cause gearchange problems. Check the shaft and drain bearing surfaces for scoring and wear and renew where necessary.

9    Renew the gearchange drain if its tracks are excessively worn. Check the contact surfaces of the drum and detent plunger for wear or damage. Check the plunger spring for fatigue or failure. Excessive wear of the stop plate will necessitate its renewal.

## 22  Examination and renovation: gearchange mechanism

1    Check for wear between the actuating arm and pins of the drum and check that each pin is a firm fit in its location. If necessary, use an impact driver to remove the drum and plate retaining screw and release the pins. Renew all the pins as a set. Check the pin retaining holes for ovality and if necessary, renew the drum.

2    Where excessive wear is found between any two bearing surfaces of the mechanism, renew the components concerned. Renew any

spring which has become fatigued or taken a set. Renew any distorted circlip.

3    Place the gearchange shaft on a sheet of plate glass and check it for straightness by attempting to insert a feeler gauge beneath it. A bent shaft will cause gearchange problems.

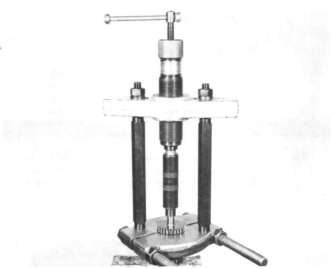

21.4 Pull the 5th gear pinion off the input shaft

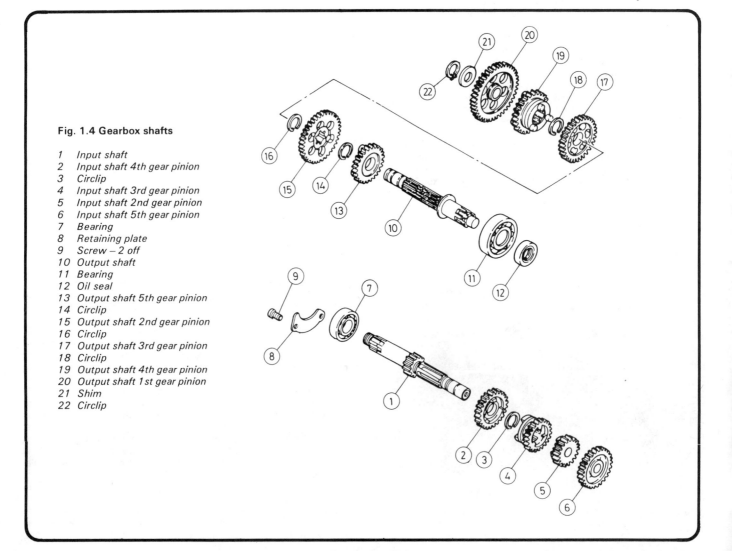

**Fig. 1.4 Gearbox shafts**

1    Input shaft
2    Input shaft 4th gear pinion
3    Circlip
4    Input shaft 3rd gear pinion
5    Input shaft 2nd gear pinion
6    Input shaft 5th gear pinion
7    Bearing
8    Retaining plate
9    Screw – 2 off
10    Output shaft
11    Bearing
12    Oil seal
13    Output shaft 5th gear pinion
14    Circlip
15    Output shaft 2nd gear pinion
16    Circlip
17    Output shaft 3rd gear pinion
18    Circlip
19    Output shaft 4th gear pinion
20    Output shaft 1st gear pinion
21    Shim
22    Circlip

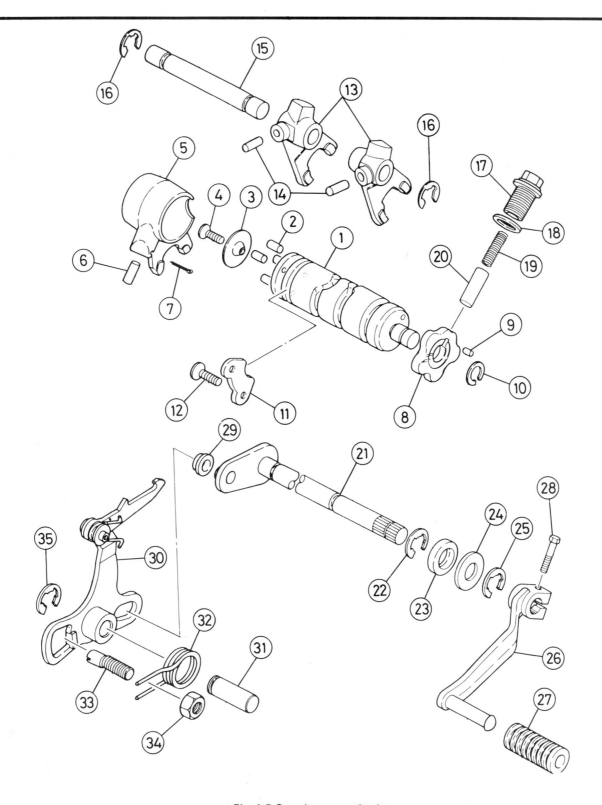

**Fig. 1.5 Gearchange mechanism**

| | | | |
|---|---|---|---|
| 1 | Gearchange drum | 10 | Circlip |
| 2 | Pin – 4 off | 11 | Stop plate |
| 3 | End plate | 12 | Screw – 2 off |
| 4 | Screw | 13 | Selector fork – 2 off |
| 5 | Selector fork | 14 | Guide pin – 2 off |
| 6 | Guide pin | 15 | Selector fork shaft |
| 7 | Split pin | 16 | Circlip – 2 off |
| 8 | Selector cam | 17 | Housing bolt |
| 9 | Locating pin | 18 | Washer |

| | | | |
|---|---|---|---|
| 19 | Spring | 27 | Rubber |
| 20 | Detent plunger | 28 | Bolt |
| 21 | Gearchange shaft | 29 | Stepped spacer |
| 22 | Circlip – MX models only | 30 | Gearchange selector arm |
| 23 | Oil seal | 31 | Selector arm shaft |
| 24 | Washer | 32 | Centralising spring |
| 25 | Circlip | 33 | Adjusting screw |
| 26 | Gearchange pedal | 34 | Locknut |
| | | 35 | Circlip |

## 23 Examination and renovation: clutch and primary drive

1    Clean the clutch components in a petrol/paraffin mix whilst observing the necessary fire precautions. Renew the O-ring fitted to the drum.

2    Overworn friction plates will cause clutch slip. Measure the thickness of each plate and renew it if the thickness is less than the limit given in Specifications.

3    Check the friction plate tangs and the drum slots for indentations caused by clutch chatter. If slight, the damage can be removed with a fine file, otherwise renewal is necessary.

4    Check all plates for distortion. Lay each one on a sheet of plate glass and attempt to insert a feeler gauge beneath it. Refer to Specifications for maximum allowable warpage.

5    Inspect each plain plate for scoring and signs of overheating in the form of blueing. Check the plate thickness with that given in Specifications. Remove slight damage to the plate tangs and hub slots with a fine file, otherwise renewal is necessary.

6    Examine the pressure plate for cracks and overheating. Look for hairline cracks around the base of each spring location and around the centre boss. Check for excessive distortion.

7    Measure the free length of each spring and renew all of them if one has set to less than the limit given in Specifications. All springs must be of equal length.

8    Any wear or scoring of the thrust washers and drum centre bush will necessitate their renewal. Check each push rod for straightness; the bend limit is 0.15 mm (0.006 in).

9    On DT50 M models, check the cushion rings for damage or wear and renew if necessary.

10   The operating mechanism is secured in the left-hand crankcase cover by a single screw. Check each part for wear and renew as necessary. Grease during assembly.

11   Examine the primary drive pinion key and its keyways in the crankshaft and pinion for wear or damage. Renew the key if necessary but before rejecting either the pinion or shaft, consult an engineering firm as to the possibilities of recutting a keyway to a larger size. Do not fit a new key to a worn keyway.

12   The drive pinion spacer should not normally suffer damage. Examine the teeth of both drive and driven pinions for excessive wear or damage. Both sets of teeth will have worn in unison and should be renewed as a matched pair, the driven pinion being part of the clutch drum.

## 24 Examination and renovation: kickstart assembly

1    Clean each part of the assembly and place it on a clean work surface. Renew any fatigued or broken springs and obviously worn or

damaged parts. The friction spring must fit firmly over the drive pinion.

2    The teeth of the drive pinion will wear in unison with those of the idler and driven pinions. In the case of excessive wear, renew the pinions as a set. The driven pinion is effectively part of the clutch drum.

3    Examine the teeth of the shaft for wear and damage and, if necessary renew the shaft and drive pinion together.

## 25 Examination and renovation: oil pump assembly

1    The oil pump is effectively a sealed unit, no replacement parts being available. Examination is limited to cleaning the unit body and checking it for hairline cracks around the screw holes and other stress points.

2    The pump drive is fitted in the right-hand crankcase cover. Damage to this assembly will be obvious. Check for excessive wear of the pinion teeth and slack between the shaft and cover. If necessary, remove the assembly by releasing the circlip and pulling the pinion and washer from the shaft. Remove the drive pin and washer to release the shaft.

3    If the shaft worm drive is damaged, then suspect damage to the drive within the pump.

23.4 Check the clutch plates for distortion

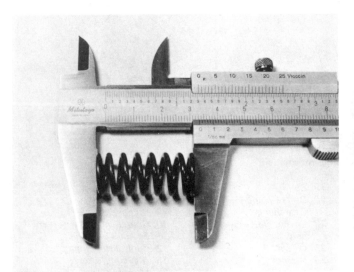

23.7 Measure clutch spring free length

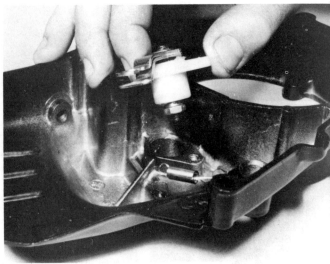

23.10 Examine the clutch operating mechanism

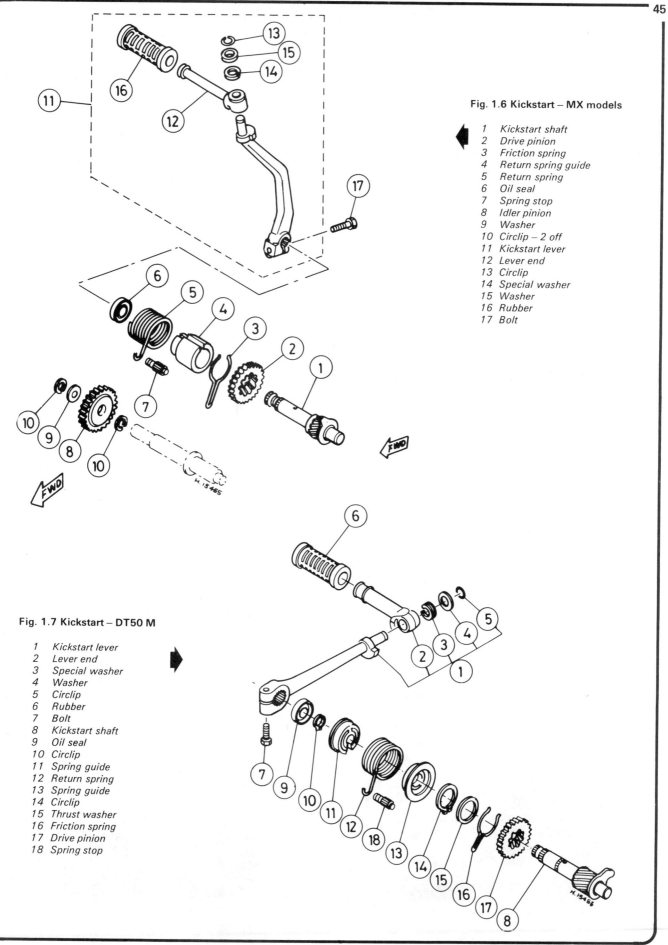

Fig. 1.6 Kickstart – MX models

1 Kickstart shaft
2 Drive pinion
3 Friction spring
4 Return spring guide
5 Return spring
6 Oil seal
7 Spring stop
8 Idler pinion
9 Washer
10 Circlip – 2 off
11 Kickstart lever
12 Lever end
13 Circlip
14 Special washer
15 Washer
16 Rubber
17 Bolt

Fig. 1.7 Kickstart – DT50 M

1 Kickstart lever
2 Lever end
3 Special washer
4 Washer
5 Circlip
6 Rubber
7 Bolt
8 Kickstart shaft
9 Oil seal
10 Circlip
11 Spring guide
12 Return spring
13 Spring guide
14 Circlip
15 Thrust washer
16 Friction spring
17 Drive pinion
18 Spring stop

## 26 Engine reassembly: general

1   Thoroughly clean each component. Avoid damaging mating surfaces when removing all gaskets or sealing compound. Carefully separate gaskets from components with a scalpel or finely honed chisel. Remove stubborn remnants of gasket and sealing compound by soaking with methylated spirits or a similar solvent. Use a soft brass-wire brush to scrub off non-hardening compounds.
2   Place the components on a clean surface near the working area together with all new gaskets and seals and any new parts. Check that nothing is missing.
3   Lay out all necessary tools. Fill an oil can with clean SAE 10W/30 oil; each moving component should be lubricated during assembly. Wipe clean the assembly area.
4   Observe all torque and clearance settings during assembly.
5   Renew all damaged fasteners. Where screw heads have been damaged, it is worth considering a set of Allen screws as a more robust replacement.

## 27 Reassembling the engine/gearbox unit: assembling the gearbox components

1   Refer to the accompanying figures and photographs when assembling the gear clusters. Clean and lubricate each component before fitting.
2   Seat each circlip properly in its groove and align the gap between its ends with the base of one of the spline channels, as shown.
3   Before pressing the 5th gear pinion over the input shaft, degrease the two mating surfaces. Check that the gap between the 5th and 2nd gear pinions is correct. Where an hydraulic press is not available, use a socket and vice to press the pinion onto the shaft. Refer to the accompanying photograph and keep the pinion square to the shaft.

## 28 Reassembling the engine/gearbox unit: refitting the crankcase components and joining the crankcase halves

1   If necessary, refit any bearing retaining plate, coating the threads of its screws with locking compound. Grease the lip of each oil seal.
2   Support the right-hand crankcase half on wooden blocks. Postion the crankshaft squarely in the main bearing, align the connecting rod with the crankcase mouth and push sharply down to seat the shaft. If necessary, tap the shaft into position, using a length of thick-walled

tube placed over its end. Do not use excessive force, and support the flywheels at a pivot opposite the crankpin to prevent distortion.
3   Lubricate the main and gearbox bearings and fit the complete gearbox assembly into the right-hand crankcase half as one unit, taking care to retain any thrust washers.
4   Check that all components are correctly aligned and refit the circlip to retain the output shaft in the crankcase. Refit the stop plate to the drum end, coating the threads of its screws with locking compound. Lubricate the gearbox components.
5   Degrease the mating surface of each crankcase half. Press the two locating dowels into the right-hand half and coat the mating surface of the same half with a thin application of sealing compound.
6   Lower the left-hand crankcase half over the shaft ends, aligning each one with its location. Press the crankcase halves together, using hand pressure. If necessary, tap around the left-hand half with a soft-faced hammer to bring the mating surfaces together. Do not use excessive force.
7   Fit the crankcase securing screws in their previously noted locations. Use an impact driver to tighten the screws and work in a diagonal sequence to prevent distortion. Wipe away excess sealing compound.
8   Check that the crank and gearbox shafts rotate freely. Investigate any tightness.

27.1a Select the gearbox output shaft ...

27.1b ... fit the 5th gear pinion and circlip ...

27.1c ... the 2nd gear pinion and circlip ...

27.1d ... the 3rd gear pinion and circlip ...

27.1e ... the 4th gear pinion ...

27.1f ... and the 1st gear pinion, thrustwasher and circlip

27.1g Select the gearbox input shaft ...

27.1h ... fit the 4th gear pinion and circlip ...

27.1i ... the 3rd gear pinion ...

27.1j ... and the 2nd gear pinion

27.3 Press the 5th gear pinion onto the input shaft

28.3a Fit the selector forks and shaft to the gearbox output shaft ...

28.3b ... fit the selector fork and drum to the input shaft ...

28.3c ... fit the gearbox assembly into the casing ...

28.4 ... and fit the output shaft retaining circlip

28.6 Press the crankcase halves together

29.1a Fit the gearchange shaft (with circlip – MX only) ...

## 29 Reassembling the engine/gearbox unit: refitting the gearchange

1 On MX models, check the circlip is correctly fitted to the gearchange shaft. Lubricate the shaft and fit it through the crankcase. Fit the washer and retaining circlip. Fit the stepped spacer to the shaft area.

2 Fit the selector arm to its pivot. Locate the legs of the return spring one on each side of the adjuster, align the arm over the spacer on the shaft arm and engage the actuating arm with the drum. Fit the retaining circlip.

3 Refer to the accompanying figure and check the clearances shown between the actuating arm and pins. If necessary, equalise the clearances by loosening the adjuster locknut and turning the adjuster. Re-lock the adjuster on completion.

4 Refit the detent plunger with its new sealing washer.

29.1b ... fit the shaft retaining clip ...

29.1c ... and fit the stepped spacer

29.2 Fit the gear selector mechanism

29.4 Fit the detent plunger

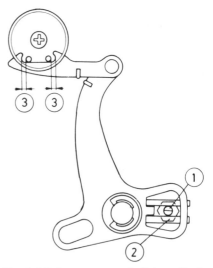

Fig. 1.8 Selector arm centralising adjustment

1   *Adjusting screw*          3   *Actuating arm to pin clearance*
2   *Locknut*

## 30  Reassembling the engine/gearbox unit: refitting the flywheel generator

1    Relocate the stator in its previously noted position and tighten its retaining screws. Clip the electrical leads to the crankcase and reconnect the neutral indicator switch.
2    Degrease the rotor and crankshaft mating surfaces. Insert the Woodruff key into the crankshaft and push the rotor over it. Gently tap the rotor centre with a soft-faced hammer to seat it and fit the plate washer, spring washer and nut. Lock the crankshaft and tighten the nut to the specified torque loading.

## 31  Reassembling the engine/gearbox unit: refitting the kickstart, primary drive pinion and clutch

1    On DT50 M models, fit the plain washer and wave washer over the gearbox output shaft. Fit the kickstart idler pinion, plate washer and circlip.

2    Fit the kickstart assembly. Align the friction spring with its crankcase slot and the teeth of the drive and idler pinions before pushing the assembly fully home. Use a stout pair of pliers to tension the return spring and hook it over its stop.
3    Fit the drive pinion spacer collar, the Woodruff key, pinion, lock washer and nut. Lock the crankshaft and tighten the nut to the specified torque loading.
4    Insert the two lengths of clutch pushrod and the ball bearing into the gearbox input shaft. Check the groove in the left-hand length is nearest the centre.
5    Fit the thrust washer and drum centre bush. Lubricate the drum centre and fit the drum, second thrust washer and the hub. Employ the method used for removal to lock the hub, fit the lock washer and nut and tighten the nut to the specified torque loading.
6    Fit the cushion rings (where fitted), plain and friction plates and the pressure plate. Fit the springs and bolts with washers. Avoid distortion of the pressure plate by tightening the bolts evenly and in a diagonal sequence. Check the new O-ring is correctly fitted around the drum.

30.1 Align the stator assembly

30.2 Torque load the rotor retaining nut

31.1 Fit the kickstart idler pinion, plate washer and circlip

31.2a Fit the kickstart drive pinion to the shaft ...

31.2b ... locate the return spring in the shaft ...

31.2c ... and fit the kickstart in the crankcase

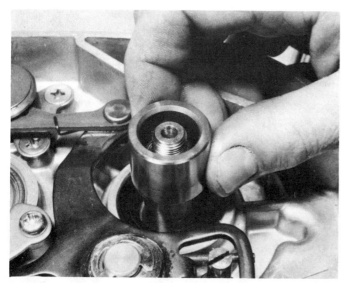

31.3a Fit the primary drive pinion spacer ...

31.3b ... fit the Woodruff key ...

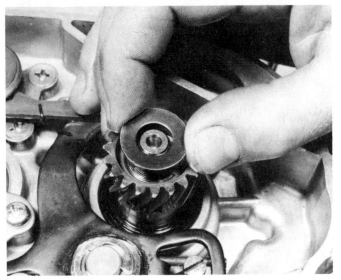

31.3c ... place a new lock washer over the pinion before fitting its retaining nut

31.4a Insert the left-hand length of clutch pushrod ...

31.4b ... drop the ball bearing into the input shaft ...

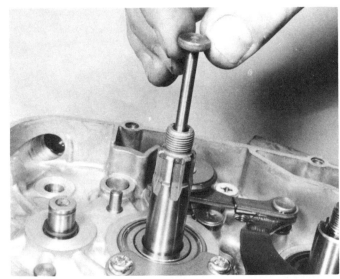

31.4c ... and insert the second length of pushrod

31.5a Fit the thrust washer and clutch drum centre bush ...

31.5b ... fit the clutch drum and second washer

31.6a Fit the plain and friction plates ...

31.6b ... the pressure plate and clutch springs

31.6c Check the O-ring is correctly fitted to the drum

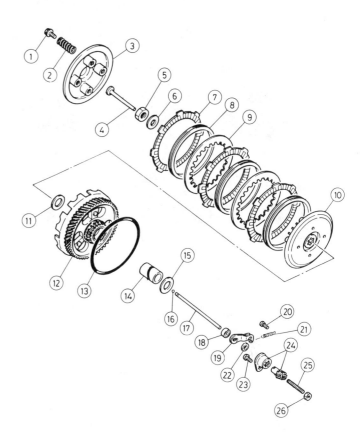

**Fig. 1.9 Clutch**

| | |
|---|---|
| 1    Bolt – 4 off | 14   Bush |
| 2    Spring – 4 off | 15   Thrust washer |
| 3    Pressure plate | 16   Ball bearing |
| 4    Pushrod | 17   Push rod |
| 5    Nut | 18   Oil seal |
| 6    Lock washer | 19   Operating arm |
| 7    Friction plate – 3 off | 20   Spring anchor |
| 8    Cushion ring – 3 off | 21   Spring |
|       DT50 M and DT80 MX only | 22   Oil seal |
| 9    Plain plate – 2 off | 23   Screw |
| 10   Hub | 24   Worm drive and housing |
| 11   Thrust washer | 25   Adjusting screw |
| 12   Drum | 26   Locknut |
| 13   O-ring | |

## 32  Reassembling the engine/gearbox unit: refitting the right-hand crankcase cover and oil pump

1    Check all components within the cover are properly fitted and lubricated. Grease the splined end of the kickstart shaft and the lip of the cover oil seal.
2    Degrease the cover and crankcase mating surfaces, press the locating dowels into the crankcase and locate the new gasket over them. Push the cover over the dowels, tapping it lightly with a soft-faced hammer to seat it properly. Align the pump drive and primary drive pinion.
3    Fit each screw into its previously noted position. Tighten the screws evenly whilst working in a diagonal sequence.
4    Clean the pump and cover mating surfaces and fit a new base gasket to the pump. Reconnect the oil feed and delivery pipes and align the pump over its drive shaft. Fit the pump retaining screws. Check the pipes are not twisted.
5    Fit the kickstart lever in its previously noted position and tighten its clamp bolt.

32.1a Fit the oil pump drive shaft ...

32.1b ... the plate washer and shaft retaining pin ...

32.1c ... align the drive pinion over the pin ...

32.1d ... and fit the retaining washer and circlip

32.1e Fit the oil scraper ...

32.2 ... and fit the right-hand crankcase cover

32.4 Clip the oil feed and delivery pipes to the pump

## 33 Reassembling the engine/gearbox unit: refitting the piston, cylinder barrel and head

1   Lubricate the big-end bearing and pack the crankcase mouth with clean rag. Lubricate and fit the small-end bearing. With the arrow cast in the piston crown facing forward, place the piston over the rod and fit the gudgeon pin. If necessary, warm the piston to aid fitting.
2   Retain the gudgeon pin with new circlips. Check each clip is correctly located; if allowed to work loose it will cause serious damage.
3   Check the piston rings are still correctly fitted. Clean the barrel and crankcase mating surfaces and fit the new base gasket. Lubricate the piston rings and cylinder bore. Lower the barrel over its retaining studs and ease the piston into the bore, carefully squeezing the ring ends together. Do not use excessive force.
4   Remove the rag from the crankcase mouth and push the barrel down onto the crankcase. Clean the barrel to head mating surfaces and fit a new head gasket. Fit the head and its retaining nuts with washers. Tighten the nuts evenly and in a diagonal sequence to the specified torque loading.
5   Reconnect the oil feed pipe to the inlet stub; check it is not twisted. Clean the carburettor to inlet stub mating surfaces, position serviceable gasket(s) between them and refit the carburettor.

33.1a Fit the small-end bearing

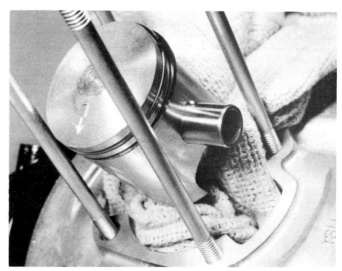

33.1b Fit the piston and gudgeon pin

33.2 Fit new gudgeon pin retaining circlips

33.3 Fit a new base gasket and the cylinder barrel

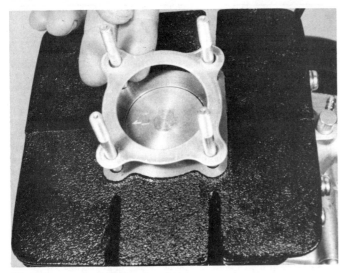

33.4a Fit a new cylinder head gasket

33.4b Tighten the cylinder head nuts correctly

### 34 Refitting the engine/gearbox unit into the frame

1   Check that no part has been omitted during reassembly. Prepare the machine and ease the engine into position from the right-hand side. Align the engine and fit the mounting bolts and nuts; tighten these to the specified torque loading.
2   Where applicable, fit the sump guard over its mounting rubbers and tighten its retaining bolts.
3   Refit the sprocket and chain over the gearbox output shaft. On MX models, fit a serviceable retaining clip. Otherwise, fit a new lock washer, lock the shaft and tighten the nut to the specified torque loading. Lock the nut by bending the lock washer against it.
4   Check the final drive chain tension, see Routine Maintenance.
5   Reconnect the clutch cable to the operating mechanism in the left-hand crankcase cover and to the handlebar lever bracket. Clean the cover and crankcase mating surfaces and press the two locating dowels into the crankcase. Fit the inner cover to the crankcase, tightening its screws evenly and in a diagonal sequence.
6   Fit the gearchange lever in its previously noted position and tighten the clamp bolt. Reconnect the generator leads and clip them to the frame.
7   Check tighten the spark plug, it must have a crash washer fitted. Reconnect the suppressor cap. Route the HT lead so that it cannot chafe on engine or frame.
8   Reconnect the inlet hose to the carburettor and tighten its clamp. If necessary, smear the hose lip with washing up liquid to aid insertion.
9   Carefully insert the throttle valve assembly into the carburettor and tighten the top of the mixing chamber. Do not use excessive force.
10  Reconnect the oil pump operating cable to the pump pulley, routing it through the cover. Fit the cable retaining clip through the pulley.
11  Refit the exhaust system. Locate a new seal between pipe and barrel and fit the mountings loosely. Tighten the exhaust port fasteners first, then the remaining mountings.
12  Reconnect the oil feed pipe to the tank and refill the tank with 2-stroke oil. Check the oil pipe connections for leaks.
13  Reconnect the battery. Check the terminals are clean and prevent corrosion occurring by smearing them with petroleum jelly. Connect the earth lead to the negative (-) terminal. Route the vent pipe clear of the lower frame.
14  Refit the fuel tank, checking there is no metal-to-metal contact which will split the tank. Reconnect the fuel feed pipe, turn on the tap and check for leaks. Fuel leaks must be cured otherwise fire may result, causing serious personal injury. On MX models, re-route the filler cap breather pipe.
15  Refit each sidepanel and secure the seat. Fit the gearbox oil drain plug with its sealing washer and tighten to the specified torque loading. Remove the filler plug and replenish the gearbox with the specified quantity of SAE 10W/30 oil, see Chapter 2.

16  Recheck each disturbed component for security. Check each control for smooth movement over its full separating range. Refer to Routine Maintenance and carry out the following:

   a)  Clutch adjustment
   b)  Throttle cable adjustment
   c)  Oil pump cable adjustment
   d)  Contact breaker adjustment and timing check

17  Refit the generator rotor cover. Select neutral and spin the crankshaft several times to prise the oil pump. Read the pump bleeding and minimum stroke procedures in Routine Maintenance.

### 35 Starting and running the rebuilt engine

1   Attempt to start the engine. Some coaxing may be necessary at first but if unsuccessful, check the plug for fouling. If problems persist, consult Fault Diagnosis.
2   Upon starting, run the engine slowly and bleed the oil pump. Open the choke as soon as possible. Any oil used during reassembly will soon burn away.
3   Check the oil pump minimum stroke and refit the pump cover.
4   Warm the engine thoroughly and check for blowing gaskets and oil leaks. Check all gears select properly and controls function correctly.

### 36 Taking the rebuilt machine on the road

1   Give the machine time to settle down by treating it gently for the first few miles. If rebored, the engine will have to be run in. This means greater use of the gearbox and a restraining hand on the throttle for at least 500 miles. Keep a light loading on the engine and gradually work up performance until this limit is reached. Where only a new crankshaft is fitted, carry out these recommendations to a lesser extent.
2   If a lubrication failure is suspected, immediately stop and investigate otherwise irreparable engine damage is inevitable.
3   Do not add oil to the petrol. This will only create excess smoke and accelerate the rate of carbon build-up in the combustion chamber and exhaust. The oil pump will provide full lubrication.
4   Do not tamper with the exhaust system or remove the silencer baffle. Doing this will decrease engine performance, as will removing the air filter.
5   After the initial run, allow the engine to cool and check all components for security. Re-adjust any controls which may have settled down.

34.5a Reconnect the clutch cable to the operating mechanism ...

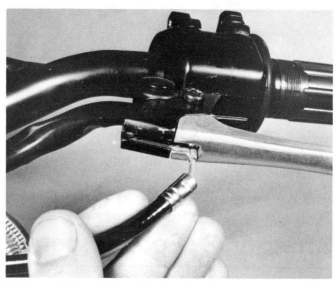

34.5b ... and also to the handlebar lever bracket

34.10 Fit the oil pump cable retaining clip

# Chapter 2 Fuel system and lubrication

## Contents

## Specifications

### Fuel tank

| | DT50 M | DT50 MX | DT80 MX |
|---|---|---|---|
| Total capacity | 6.0 litre (1.32 Imp gal) | 8.5 litre (1.87 Imp gal) | 8.5 litre (1.87 Imp gal) |

### Carburettor

| | DT50 M | DT50 MX | DT80 MX 1981 | DT80 MX 1982 and 1983 |
|---|---|---|---|---|
| Make | Mikuni | Teikei | Teikei | Mikuni |
| Type | VM16SH | Y14P | Y16P | VM18SS |
| ID No | 2K000 | 5M600 | 5J100 | 12X00 |
| Main jet | 70 | 88 | 102 | 120 |
| Needle jet | E2 | 2.080 | 2.085 | E2 |
| Jet needle | 303-2 | 059-2 | 3N20-4 | 4J33-3 |
| Pilot jet | 20 | 40 | 36 | 20 |
| Pilot air screw setting (turns out) | 2 | $1\frac{1}{2}$ | $1\frac{1}{4}$ | $1\frac{1}{8}$ |
| Air jet | 2.5 | 2.5 | 2.5 | 2.5 |
| Throttle valve cutaway | 2.0 | 1.0 | 1.5 | 2.0 |
| Starter jet | 30 | N/App | N/App | 20 |
| Float height | 22.4 mm (0.88 in) | 23 ± 1.0 mm (0.91 ± 0.04 in) | 23 ± 1.0 mm (0.91 ± 0.04 in) | 19 ± 1.0 mm (0.75 ± 0.04 in) |
| Engine idling speed | 1300 rpm | 1250 rpm | 1300 rpm | 1300 rpm |

### Reed valve

| | DT50 M | DT50 MX | DT80 MX 1981 | DT80 MX 1982 and 1983 |
|---|---|---|---|---|
| Lift | 7.0 mm (0.275 in) | 8.0 mm (0.31 in) | 8.0 mm (0.31 in) | 7.0 mm (0.275 in) |
| Bend limit | 0.3 mm (0.012 in) | 0.8 mm (0.03 in) | 0.8 mm (0.03 in) | 0.3 mm (0.012 in) |

### Air cleaner

Element type .................................................... Oiled polyurethane foam

### Lubrication

Engine system .................................................. Yamaha Autolube – Pump fed total-loss system
Oil type .......................................................... Good quality non-diluent 2-stroke oil
Oil capacity .................................................... 1.0 litre (1.76 Imp pint)
Oil pump minimum stroke:
    DT50 and DT80 MX 1981 ......................... 0.20 – 0.25 mm (0.008 – 0.010 in)
    DT80 MX 1982, 83 .................................. 0.30 – 0.35 mm (0.012 – 0.014 in)

| | DT50 M | All others |
|---|---|---|
| Gearbox oil capacity: | | |
| At oil change .................................................. | 550 cc (0.97 Imp pint) | 600 cc (1.05 Imp pint) |
| At engine overhaul ......................................... | 600 cc (1.05 Imp pint) | 650 cc (1.14 Imp pint) |
| Oil type ........................................................... | SAE 10W/30 | SAE 10W/30 |

## 1 General description

Fuel is gravity fed from the tank to the carburettor float chamber via a three-position tap. Air drawn into the carburettor is filtered through an oil-impregnated foam element.

The point of induction on a two-stroke engine is normally controlled by the piston skirt, which covers and uncovers ports machined in the cylinder bore. On Yamaha DT models, a supplementary timing system, in the form of a reed valve, is incorporated to enable more efficient induction timing. The reed valve maintains an even flow of the combustion mixture and reduces the possibility of blow-back of the combustible gases, thereby contributing greatly towards an economical and powerful engine.

Engine lubrication is by Yamaha Autolube. Oil is gravity fed from the tank to a pump which is crankshaft driven and interconnected by cable to the throttle twistgrip, thus the amount of oil pumped varies according to engine speed and throttle setting.

Pumped oil is fed directly to the inlet tract where it mixes with the incoming mixture charge being drawn to the crankcase. The oil is deposited to lubricate the bearings and the cylinder bore and pistons. Residual oil enters the combustion chamber with the incoming mixture and is burnt.

Lubrication for the transmission components is by oil contained within the gearbox casing, isolated from the working parts of the engine proper.

## 2 Fuel tank: removal and refitting

1 Turn the tap lever to 'Off'. Observe the necessary fire precautions and unclip the fuel feed pipe, draining any fuel from the pipe into a clean container. On MX models, release the filler cap breather pipe.
2 Raise the seat and remove the tank retaining bolt or rubber. Pull the tank rearwards off its mounting rubbers and place it in safe storage, away from naked flame or sparks. Check for leaks around the tap and cover the tank to protect its paint finish. Renew any damaged mounting rubbers.
3 Reverse the removal procedure to fit the tank. If necessary, wipe the front mounting rubbers with petrol to ease their reinstallation. Secure the tank and check for metal-to-metal contact which might split the tank.
4 Reconnect the pipe, turn on the tap and check for leaks. Fuel leaks will waste petrol and cause a fire hazard. On MX models, re-route the filler cap breather pipe.

## 3 Fuel tap: cleaning the collector bowl and filter

1 Refer to Routine Maintenance for details of this operation.

## 4 Fuel tap: removal and refitting, and curing of leaks

1 Fuel can leak from any one of three points on the tap; the tap to tank joint, tap lever joint or collector bowl joint. If check-tightening the component fails to effect a cure, then proceed as follows.
2 Leakage of the tap to tank joint will be caused by a defective sealing ring. Observe the necessary fire precautions and drain the tank by detaching the fuel feed pipe from the carburettor and placing its end in a clean, sealable metal container. Detach the tap, taking care not to damage its filter stacks. Remove the defective sealing ring.
3 If necessary, clean each stack by rinsing in clean petrol. Remove stubborn contamination by gentle brushing with a used toothbrush or similar item soaked in petrol. Protect the eyes from spray-back from the brush.
4 A holed stack should be renewed as it will allow sediment into the tap body. Clean the tap and tank mating surfaces and fit a new sealing

ring. Refit the tap, reconnect the pipe, refill the tank and check for leaks.
5 Leakage of the lever joint will be caused by a defective seal. Drain the tank and remove the lever by releasing its retaining screw(s). On MX models, renew the O-ring, otherwise, renew the tap valve.
6 Renew the lever spring if broken or fatigued. Fit the lever, check its operation, refill the tank and check for leaks.
7 Refer to Routine Maintenance for details of the collector bowl joint.

## 5 Fuel feed pipe: examination

1 This thin-walled synthetic rubber pipe is a push-on type and need only be replaced if hard or split. Renew its retaining clips if fatigued.

4.4 Renew a damaged sealing ring or filter stack

4.7 Examine the collector bowl assembly

## 6  Carburettor: removal and refitting

1  Turn the fuel top lever to 'Off'. Observe the necessary fire precautions and unclip the fuel feed pipe from the carburettor. Unscrew the top of the carburettor mixing chamber and pull the throttle valve assembly from the chamber.

2  Detach the inlet hose from the carburettor by releasing its clamp. Renew the hose if split or perished. On DT50 M models, the sidepanels can be removed for greater access.

### DT50 M

3  Remove the two retaining bolts with spring and plain washers and carefully ease the carburettor from the inlet stub. Note the gaskets and spacer and renew the gaskets if damaged.

### DT50 MX and 80 MX

4  Release the carburettor retaining clamp and pull the carburettor from the inlet stub. Note the fitted position of the sealing rings and renew if damaged.

### All models

5  Check that any O-ring or gaskets are serviceable and correctly located. Air drawn in through a joint will badly affect engine performance. On DT50 M models, tighten the carburettor retaining bolts evenly to avoid distortion of the mating face. Check all mating faces are clean before fitting.

6  Reconnect the inlet hose and tighten its clamp. If necessary, smear the hose lip with washing up liquid to aid insertion. Carefully insert the throttle valve assembly into the mixing chamber and tighten its top; do not use excessive force.

7  Refer to Routine Maintenance and check throttle cable adjustment. Reconnect the fuel pipe, turn on the tap and check for leaks.

## 7  Carburettor: examination, renovation and reassembly

1  Cover an area of work surface with clean paper. This will prevent components placed upon it from becoming contaminated or lost.

2  Remove the float chamber retaining screws. If necessary, tap around the chamber to body joint with a soft-faced hammer to free the chamber. Remove the float pivot pin and detach the twin floats. Displace the float needle, it is very small and easily lost. Where possible, unscrew the float needle seat with sealing washer.

3  Unscrew the pilot jet, main jet and needle jet. On 1982 and '83, DT80 MX models the needle jet retainer will unscrew; push the jet

with O-ring from its location whilst noting alignment. When removing any jet, use a close fitting screwdriver of the correct type otherwise damage will occur.

4  Note the pilot air screw and throttle stop screw settings by counting the number of turns required to screw them fully in until seating lightly; this will make it easier to 'retune' the carburettor after reassembly. Remove both screws with their springs.

5  Refer to the relevant figure accompanying this text and remove the choke assembly. It is not necessary to remove the drain plug from the float chamber except for seal renewal.

6  Before examination, thoroughly clean each part in clean petrol, using a soft nylon brush to remove stubborn contamination and a compressed air jet to blow dry. Avoid using rag because lint will obstruct jet orifices. Do not use wire to clear blocked jets, this will enlarge the jet and increase petrol consumption; if an air jet fails use a soft nylon bristle. Observe the necessary fire precautions and wear eye protection against blow-back from the air jet.

7  Renew distorted or cracked casting. Renew all O-rings and gaskets. Replace fatigued or broken springs and flattened spring washers.

8  Wear of the float needle takes the form of a groove around its seating area; renew if worn. Check for similar wear of the needle seat and, if possible, renew when worn. Where fitted, check the needle end pin is free to move and is spring loaded.

9  Check the floats for damage and leakage. Renew if damaged, it is not advisable to attempt a repair.

10  Examine the choke assembly, renewing any worn or damaged parts. Renew hardened drain or fuel feed pipes.

11  Wear of the throttle valve will be denoted by polished areas on its external diameter, causing air leaks which weaken the mixture and produce erratic slow running. Examine the carburettor body for similar wear and renew each component as necessary.

12  Examine the jet needle for scratches or wear along its length and for straightness. If necessary, dismantle the valve assembly by putting the return spring against the mixing chamber top and releasing the throttle cable from the valve. Remove the needle retaining plate or clip and remove the needle from the valve.

13  Renew the seal within the mixing chamber top if damaged. The throttle return spring must be free of fatigue or corrosion.

14  Before assembly, clean all parts and place them on clean paper in a logical order. Do not use excessive force during reassembly, it is easy to shear a jet or damage a casting.

15  Reassembly is a reverse of dismantling. If in doubt, refer to the accompanying figures or photographs. Seat the pilot air and throttle stop screws lightly before screwing out to their previously noted settings. Alternatively set the pilot air screw as specified and refer to Routine Maintenance for carburettor adjustment to set the throttle stop screw.

7.7a Examine the carburettor mouth seal ...

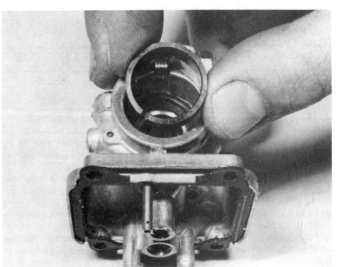

7.7b ... and fit the insulating ring (Teikei carburettor)

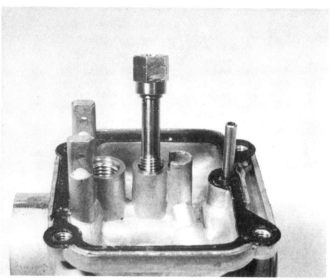

7.15a Fit the needle jet ...

7.15b ... the main jet ...

7.15c ... the pilot jet ...

7.15d ... the float needle seat with washer and the needle (Teikei carburettor)

7.15e Retain the floats with the pivot pin ...

7.15f ... fit the float chamber with gasket ...

**Fig. 2.1 Carburettor – DT50 M**

| | | | |
|---|---|---|---|
| 1 | Carburettor assembly | 18 | Locknut |
| 2 | Pilot jet | 19 | Adjusting bolt |
| 3 | Float needle seat | 20 | Rubber cover |
| 4 | Sealing washer | 21 | Pilot air screw |
| 5 | Needle jet | 22 | Spring – 2 off |
| 6 | Main jet | 23 | Throttle stop screw |
| 7 | Float | 24 | Choke plunger |
| 8 | Pivot pin | 25 | Choke control knob |
| 9 | Float chamber gasket | 26 | Split pin |
| 10 | Float chamber | 27 | Cap |
| 11 | Throttle valve | 28 | Circlip |
| 12 | Jet needle | 29 | Plunger retainer |
| 13 | Jet needle clip | 30 | Spring |
| 14 | Needle retaining clip | 31 | Vent pipe |
| 15 | Return spring | 32 | Overflow pipe |
| 16 | Sealing ring | 33 | Screw – 4 off |
| 17 | Mixing chamber top | 34 | Spring washer – 4 off |

7.15g ... fit the pilot air screw (arrowed) and throttle stop screw (Teikei carburettor)

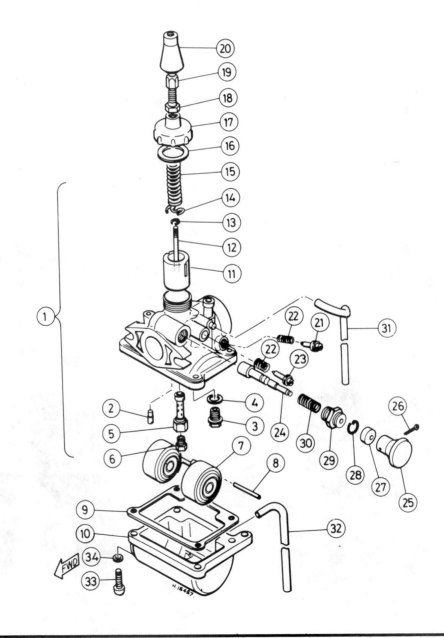

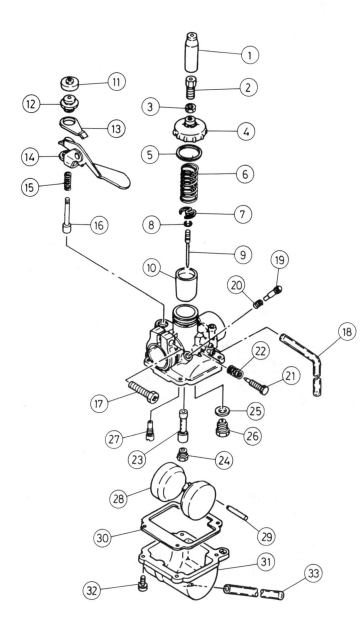

**Fig. 2.2 Carburettor – MX models**

| 1 Rubber cover | 18 Vent pipe |
|---|---|
| 2 Adjusting bolt | 19 Pilot air screw |
| 3 Locknut | 20 Spring |
| 4 Mixing chamber top | 21 Throttle stop screw |
| 5 Sealing ring | 22 Spring |
| 6 Return spring | 23 Needle jet |
| 7 Needle retaining clip | 24 Main jet |
| 8 Jet needle clip | 25 Sealing washer |
| 9 Jet needle | 26 Float needle seat |
| 10 Throttle valve | 27 Pilot jet |
| 11 Cap | 28 Float |
| 12 Plunger retainer | 29 Pivot pin |
| 13 Stopper plate | 30 Float chamber gasket |
| 14 Choke operating lever | 31 Float chamber |
| 15 Spring | 32 Screw – 4 off |
| 16 Choke plunger | 33 Overflow pipe |
| 17 Bolt | |

## 8 Carburettor: settings

1 The predetermined jet sizes, throttle valve cutaway and needle position should not require modification. Check with Specifications for standard settings. Carburettor wear occurs very slowly, therefore, if a sudden fault in engine performance occurs, check all other main systems before suspecting the carburettor.

2 The standard fitted position of the jet needle clip is indicated by the suffix number of the needle number identification. For example, 303-2 indicates the clip should be fitted in the 2nd groove down from the needle top.

3 Incorrect float height, leaking seals and defective air filter and exhaust system will all result in bad engine performance.

4 If possible, ride the machine for approximately 5 miles and stop the engine without letting it tick over. Remove the spark plug and check its electrodes and insulator for condition and colour as defined in Chapter 3. This will give a good indication of any fault in carburation.

5 As a guide, up to $\frac{1}{8}$th throttle is controlled by the pilot jet, $\frac{1}{8}$ to $\frac{1}{4}$ by the throttle valve cutaway, $\frac{1}{4}$ to $\frac{3}{4}$ by the needle position and from $\frac{3}{4}$ to full by the main jet size. These are approximate divisions which are not clear cut, there being an amount of overlap between the stages.

6 The pilot air screw setting is specified. If the engine dies at low speed, suspect a blocked pilot jet. Refer to Routine Maintenance for carburettor adjustment.

7 Settings will be affected by fitting non-standard air filters, exhaust systems, etc. Refer to the equipment manufacturer for advice.

## 9 Carburettor: checking the float height

1 Flooding of the carburettor or excessive mixture weakness will indicate incorrect float height. Remove the carburettor, invert it and remove the float chamber with gasket. Renew this gasket if damaged.

2 Place the inverted carburettor on a flat and level surface. Measure the distance from the body gasket surface to the furthest surface of the float as shown in the accompanying figure and compare the reading obtained with the figure given in Specifications. If necessary, alter the setting by bending the small tongue sited between the floats.

## 10 Carburettor: adjustment

1 Refer to Routine Maintenance for details of this operation.

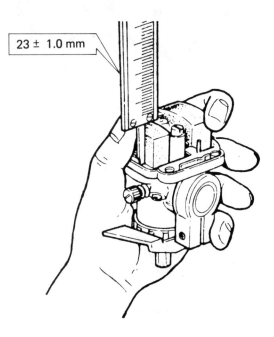

23 ± 1.0 mm

**Fig. 2.3 Checking the float height**

## 11 Reed valve: removal, examination and refitting

1   Remove the carburettor. Remove the four retaining bolts with washers and detach the inlet stub reed valve assembly, taking care not to tear the gaskets.
2   After a considerable mileage the valve reeds may lose some springiness and their performance will suffer. Check for obvious damage, such as cracked reeds. Refer to the accompanying figure and measure valve lift and bend limit. If the measurement exceeds that specified, renew the necessary valve part.
3   Before refitting the reed or inlet stub retaining screws, coat their threads with a locking compound. Damaged gaskets must be renewed. Tighten the stub retaining screws evenly to avoid distorting the valve body.

## 12 Air filter element: removal, examination, cleaning and refitting

1   Refer to Routine Maintenance for details of this operation.

## 13 Engine lubrication system: general maintenance

1   An adequate level of oil must be maintained in the tank; the sight glass will indicate a low level. Use only that oil specified.
2   Regularly check oil feed and delivery pipes for splitting or perishing. All connections must be free from leaks, which will eventually cause loss of lubrication and subsequent engine seizure.
3   Refer to Routine Maintenance for oil pump adjustment if incorrect lubrication is suspected.

## 14 Oil pump: removal and refitting

1   The pump is a sealed unit; in the event of failure it must be renewed. Remove the left-hand sidepanel. Using a bulldog clip or similar item, close the oil feed pipe from the tank.
2   Remove the pump cover from the right-hand crankcase cover. Pull the cable retaining clip from the pump pulley, detach the cable from the pulley and pull it clear.
3   Obtain a piece of absorbent rag. Remove the pump retaining screws and ease it far enough out of its housing to allow detachment of the oil feed and delivery pipes. Remove the pump and catch in the rag any oil emitting from the pipes.
4   Before fitting the pump, clean its mating surface with the cover and fit a new base gasket. Reconnect the oil feed and delivery pipes, checking they are not twisted. Align the pump over its drive shaft and fit the retaining screws.
5   Remove the clip from the oil feed pipe, replenish the oil tank and refit the sidepanel. Reconnect the pump cable and retaining clip. Refer to Routine Maintenance and carry out adjustment of the cable, bleeding of the pump and checking of its minimum stroke. Check for leaks and refit the pump cover.

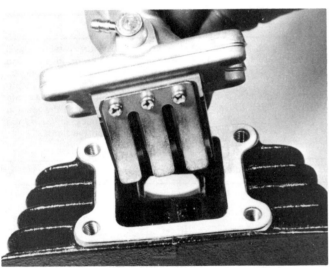

11.3a Fit the reed valve with serviceable gasket ...

11.3b ... reconnect the oil feed pipe

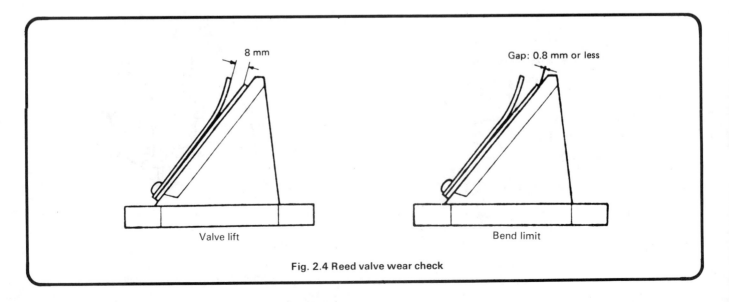

Fig. 2.4 Reed valve wear check

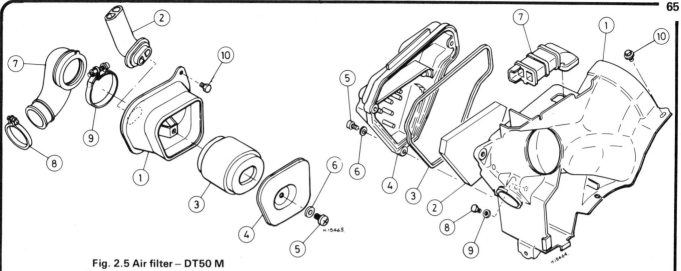

**Fig. 2.5 Air filter – DT50 M**

| 1 | Air filter casing | 6 | Washer |
|---|---|---|---|
| 2 | Air inlet hose | 7 | Air outlet hose |
| 3 | Element | 8 | Hose clamp |
| 4 | Cover | 9 | Hose clamp |
| 5 | Screw | 10 | Bolt – 2 off |

**Fig. 2.6 Air filter – MX models**

| 1 | Air filter casing | 6 | Washer – 3 off |
|---|---|---|---|
| 2 | Element | 7 | Air inlet hose |
| 3 | Casing seal | 8 | Bolt |
| 4 | Cover | 9 | Washer |
| 5 | Screw – 3 off | 10 | Bolt and washer – 4 off |

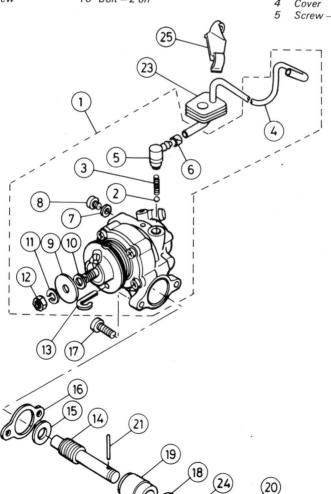

**Fig. 2.7 Oil pump**

1 Oil pump assembly
2 Steel ball
3 Spring
4 Feed pipe
5 Union
6 Spring clip
7 Sealing washer
8 Bleed screw
9 Adjustment plate
10 Shim
11 Spring washer
12 Nut
13 Clip
14 Drive shaft
15 Washer
16 Gasket
17 Screw – 2 off
18 Oil seal
19 Sleeve
20 Drive pinion
21 Locating pin
22 Circlip
23 Casing grommet
24 Washer – 2 off
25 Pipe clamp

## 15 Oil pump: bleeding of air

1    Refer to Routine Maintenance for details of this operation.

## 16 Gearbox lubrication: general maintenance

1    Maintenance of the gearbox lubrication system consists of regular checking of the oil level and changing of the oil. Refer to Routine Maintenance for details of these operations.

## 17 Exhaust system: removal and refitting

1    Remove the right-hand sidepanel. Detach the exhaust silencer from the frame and exhaust pipe. Release the pipe to cylinder barrel retaining ring and, on MX models, unbolt the pipe from the frame. Ease the pipe clear of the frame.

2    Renew flattened spring washers and damaged seals. Renew the seal between pipe and barrel.

3    Clean and examine the system and mounting components. Slight damage can be repaired by brazing a patch over the affected area. Refinish by wire brushing and degreasing the system and spraying with a suitable aerosol paint such as Sperex VHT.

4    When refitting, tighten each mounting finger-tight. Tighten the pipe to barrel ring first then the remaining mountings.

5    Treat any after-market system with caution, checking it is of reputable manufacture. Refer to the supplier for any alterations in carburettor jetting.

## 18 Exhaust system: lubrication

1    Refer to Routine Maintenance for details of this operation.

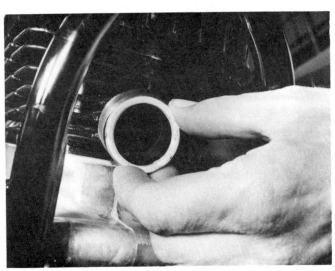

17.4a Fit a new exhaust gasket ...

17.4b ... tighten the pipe securing ring with a C-spanner

# Chapter 3  Ignition system

## Contents

## Specifications

### Ignition system
Type ...................................................................... Coil and contact breaker

### Ignition timing
Piston position BTDC ...................................................... 1.80 ± 0.15 mm (0.07 ± 0.006 in)

### Contact breaker gap ..................................................... 0.35 ± 0.05 mm (0.014 ± 0.002 in)

### Condenser capacity ...................................................... 0.25 microfarad

### Spark plug
Make ...................................................................... NGK
Type:
    DT50 M amd MX ...................................... B7HS
    DT80 MX ............................................ B8HS
Electrode gap ............................................................. 0.6 mm (0.024 in)

### Ignition coil

| | DT50 M | DT50 MX and 80 MX |
|---|---|---|
| Primary winding resistance | 1.02 ohm ± 10% | 1.0 ohm ± 15% |
| Secondary winding resistance | 6.0 K ohm ± 20% | 5.9 K ohm ± 15% |

### Flywheel generator

| | | |
|---|---|---|
| Ignition source coil resistance | 1.35 ohm ± 10% | 1.64 ohm ± 10% |

## 1  General description

A conventional contact breaker ignition system is fitted. As the generator rotor moves, alternating current (ac) is generated in the ignition source coil of the stator. With the contact breaker closed, the current runs to earth. When the breaker opens, the current transfers to the ignition coil primary windings. A high voltage is thus produced in the coil secondary windings (by mutual induction) and fed to the spark plug via the HT lead.

As energy flows to earth across the plug electrodes, a spark is produced and the combustible gases in the cylinder ignited. A condenser prevents arcing across the breaker points which helps reduce erosion due to burning.

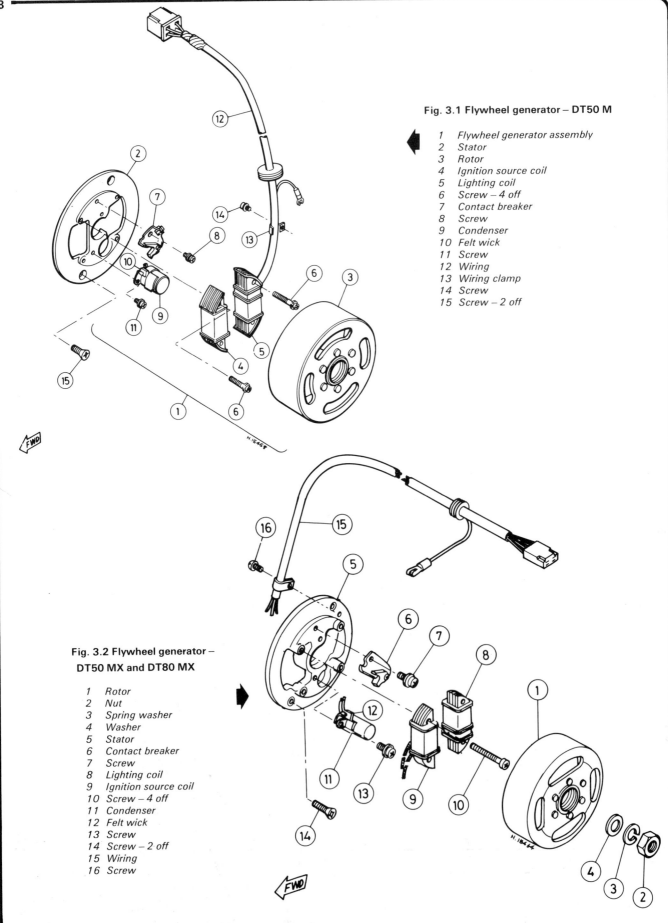

**Fig. 3.1 Flywheel generator – DT50 M**

1 Flywheel generator assembly
2 Stator
3 Rotor
4 Ignition source coil
5 Lighting coil
6 Screw – 4 off
7 Contact breaker
8 Screw
9 Condenser
10 Felt wick
11 Screw
12 Wiring
13 Wiring clamp
14 Screw
15 Screw – 2 off

**Fig. 3.2 Flywheel generator –**
**DT50 MX and DT80 MX**

1 Rotor
2 Nut
3 Spring washer
4 Washer
5 Stator
6 Contact breaker
7 Screw
8 Lighting coil
9 Ignition source coil
10 Screw – 4 off
11 Condenser
12 Felt wick
13 Screw
14 Screw – 2 off
15 Wiring
16 Screw

**Spark plug maintenance:** Checking plug gap with feeler gauges

Altering the plug gap. Note use of correct tool

**Spark plug conditions:** A brown, tan or grey firing end is indicative of correct engine running conditions and the selection of the appropriate heat rating plug

White deposits have accumulated from excessive amounts of oil in the combustion chamber or through the use of low quality oil. Remove deposits or a hot spot may form

Black sooty deposits indicate an over-rich fuel/air mixture, or a malfunctioning ignition system. If no improvement is obtained, try one grade hotter plug

Wet, oily carbon deposits form an electrical leakage path along the insulator nose, resulting in a misfire. The cause may be a badly worn engine or a malfunctioning ignition system

A blistered white insulator or melted electrode indicates over-advanced ignition timing or a malfunctioning cooling system. If correction does not prove effective, try a colder grade plug

A worn spark plug not only wastes fuel but also overloads the whole ignition system because the increased gap requires higher voltage to initiate the spark. This condition can also affect air pollution

## 2   Contact breaker: gap setting and timing check

1   Refer to Routine Maintenance for details of these operations.

## 3   Contact breaker: removal, renovation and refitting

1   Remove the contact breaker points for dressing if they are burned, pitted or badly worn. Renew them if a substantial amount of material has to be removed.
2   Remove the gearchange lever, noting its fitted position. Remove the outer and inner covers from the left-hand crankcase.
3   Prevent crankshaft rotation by selecting top gear and applying the rear brake. Alternatively, fit a strap wrench around the generator rotor. Remove the rotor retaining nut, spring washer and plate washer. Pull the rotor from the crankshaft as shown in Chapter 1 and remove the Woodruff key.
4   Disconnect the electrical lead from the spring blade of the moving point and remove the blade securing screw. Remove the clip and lift the moving contact from its pivot pin. Note the fitted position of any insulating washers. Remove the fixed contact securing screw to release the contact from the stator plate.
5   Dress the points surfaces by rubbing them on an oilstone or fine emery paper, keeping them square to the abrasive. Remove all traces of abrasive.
6   When reassembling, refit all insulating washers correctly to prevent inadvertent earthing of the assembly which will render it inoperative. Grease the pivot pin sparingly and apply a few drops of oil to the cam lubricating wick.
7   Excessive burning of the contacts can be caused by a faulty condenser, refer to the following Section.
8   With the contact breaker assembly and rotor fitted, refer to Routine Maintenance for points adjustment and timing check.

## 4   Condenser: testing, removal and refitting

1   The condenser prevents arcing across the contact breaker points as they separate; it is connected in parallel with the points. If misfiring occurs or starting proves difficult, it is possible that the condenser is faulty. To check, separate the points by hand with the ignition on. If the points spark excessively and appear burnt, the condenser is unserviceable.
2   No test is possible without the appropriate equipment. Check by substitution, a replacement is cheap. Refer to the preceding Section and remove the generator rotor. Disconnect the stator wiring and note the fitted position of the stator before removing its retaining screws.
3   Disconnect the condenser's leads and remove its securing screw. Rotate and connect each lead correctly when fitting the new condenser. With the generator refitted, refer to Routine Maintenance for breaker adjustment and timing check.

## 5   Flywheel generator: output check

1   The flywheel generator provides power for the ignition system. Failure or malfunction of the source coil will affect system operation. If there is no evidence of a spark at the plug electrodes and the machine will not start, refer to Chapter 6 for the test procedure but before doing this check that all component parts of the system are serviceable and, where applicable, correctly adjusted. Check the circuit wiring for chafing or breakage and that all connections are correctly made and free of corrosion.

## 6   Ignition coil: testing

1   Note that a defective condenser can give the illusion of a defective coil, refer to Section 4 before condemning the coil.
2   Remove the fuel tank, pull the suppressor cap from the spark plug and disconnect the coil low tension (LT) lead.
3   Set a multimeter to its resistance function (K ohm). Connect one meter probe to the suppressor cap connection and the other probe to earth. The meter reading should equal that given in Specifications if the secondary windings of the coil are serviceable.
4   Reset the meter to its ohms scale. Connect one probe to the LT lead and the other to earth. Compare the meter reading with that specified for the primary windings of the coil.
5   An open or short circuit in the coil windings will necessitate coil renewal. If in doubt, have a Yamaha agent test the coil on a spark gap tester.

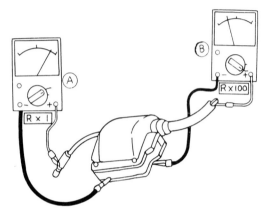

**Fig. 3.3 Ignition coil resistance test**

*A   Primary coil test*     *B   Secondary coil test*

## 7   Spark plug: checking and resetting the gap

1   Refer to Routine Maintenance for details of this operation.

## 8   High tension lead: examination

1   Erratic running faults can sometimes be attributed to leakage from the HT lead and spark plug. With this fault, it will often be possible to see tiny sparks around the lead and suppressor cap at night. One cause is dampness and the accumulation of road salts around the lead. It is often possible to cure the problem by drying and cleaning the components and spraying them with an aerosol ignition sender.
2   If the system has become swamped with water, use a water dispersant spray. Renew the cap seals if defective. If the lead or cap are suspected of breaking down internally, renew the component.
3   Where the lead is permanently attached to the ignition coil, entrust its renewal to an auto-electrician who will have the expertise to solder on a new lead without damaging the coil windings.

# Chapter 4 Frame and forks

## Contents

## Specifications

| | DT50 M | DT50 MX and 80 MX |
|---|---|---|
| **Frame** | | |
| Type .................................................... | Cradle, welded tubular steel | |
| **Front forks** | | |
| Type ..................................................... | Oil damped telescopic | Oil damped telescopic |
| Travel ................................................... | 110 mm (4.33 in) | 160 mm (6.30 mm) |
| Spring free length ............................... | N/Av | 385.5 mm (15.18 in) |
| Oil capacity (per leg) ........................... | 140 cc | 208 cc |
| | (4.93 Imp fl oz) | (7.32 Imp fl oz) |
| Oil type ................................................ | SAE 10W/30 motor oil | SAE 10 fork oil |
| **Rear suspension** | | |
| Type ..................................................... | Swinging arm fork controlled by two suspension units | Swinging arm subframe controlled by single suspension unit |
| Travel: | | |
| At suspension unit ............................. | N/Av | 65 mm (2.56 in) |
| At wheel spindle ............................... | N/Av | 130 mm (5.12 in) |
| **Rear suspension unit** | | |
| Type ..................................................... | Coil spring, oil damper | Gas/coil spring, oil damper |
| Spring free length ............................... | N/Av | 223 mm (8.78 in) |
| Service limit ........................................ | N/Av | 210 mm (8.27 in) |
| **Torque wrench settings – kgf m (lbf ft)** | **DT50 M** | **DT50 MX and 80 MX** |
| Headlamp clamp bolts ......................... | N/Av | 2.0 (14.5) |
| Steering stem top bolt ........................ | 6.0 (43.3) | 6.5 (47.0) |
| Upper yoke pinch bolts ....................... | 2.5 (18.0) | 2.6 (18.8) |
| Lower yoke pinch bolts ....................... | 2.5 (18.0) | 3.2 (23.1) |
| Swinging arm pivot shaft nut ............... | 2.5 (18.0) | 4.2 (30.4) |
| Rear suspension unit securing nuts ....................... | 3.5 (25.3) | N/Av |

## 1 General description

The frame is of conventional welded tubular steel construction. DT50 M models have a full duplex cradle design whereas MX models have a single front downtube which divides into a duplex cradle at its base.

The front forks are the conventional telescopic type, having internal oil-filled damping.

DT50 M models have conventional swinging arm rear suspension, controlled by two oil-filled suspension units which provide the necessary damping.

MX models are equipped with Yamaha Monocross suspension incorporating a fabricated subframe which pivots on the main frame whilst being controlled by a single gas/oil suspension unit.

## 2   Front fork legs: removal and refitting

1    Refer to Chapter 5 and remove the front wheel.
2    Slacken each fork yoke pinch bolt. On DT50 M models, release each headlamp bracket clamp bolt. Pull each leg downwards to clear the fork yokes.
3    When fitting the legs and wheel, tighten each nut or bolt finger-tight. Align the top of each stanchion with the top surface of the upper yoke. Fully tighten each nut or bolt to the specified torque loading, starting with the wheel spindle nut and working upwards.

## 3   Front fork legs: dismantling, examination, renovation and reassembly

1    Dismantle each leg separately, using an identical procedure. This will prevent parts being unwittingly exchanged between legs. Refer to the accompanying figure when dismantling and lay out the component parts in order of removal.
2    With the leg vertical, clamp its stanchion between the protected jaws of a vice. Remove the top bolt, washer and O-ring. Invert the leg over a suitable container and pump the lower leg up and down the stanchion to assist draining of the oil.

### DT50 M
3    Detach the dust seal. Clamp the lower leg between the protected jaws of a vice and use a strap wrench to unscrew the tube nut from the leg. Pull the stanchion out of the lower leg; if necessary, jerk the stanchion sharply to displace the bush. Remove the spring, washer and spacer from the stanchion. Displace the O-ring and oil seal from the tube nut, taking care not to damage the nut.

### DT50 MX and 80 MX
4    Release the gaiter retaining clamp and remove the gaiter. Using a small screwdriver, carefully remove the oil seal retaining clip and washer.
5    With the leg horizontal, clamp the wheel spindle boss between the protected jaws of a vice. Repeatedly pull the stanchion sharply outwards to displace the oil seal and bush from the lower leg. Withdraw the stanchion. Remove the spring, washer and spacer from the stanchion. The washer has flats on its outer edge which must be aligned with the stanchion before removal. Check the circlip on the stanchion for damage and renew if necessary.

### All models
6    Check the stanchion for straightness by rolling it on a flat surface. A bent stanchion or one with peeling chrome plate must be renewed.

Ease down high spots on the stanchion outer surface to avoid damaging the oil seal during reassembly.
7    If wear exists between the bush and stanchion or lower leg, renew the bush. Wear of the stanchion will be indicated by scuffing and penetration of its chromed surface.
8    Measure the spring length and compare it with that specified or with a new spring. If a spring has taken a permanent set to a shorter length, renew both springs as a set. Check the spring spacer and washer for wear and renew if necessary.
9    Renew the oil seal and O-ring(s) as a matter of course. Renew the gaiter or dust seal if split or perished. It is a good idea to protect the exposed stanchions of the DT50 M by fitting gaiters instead of the standard dust seals.
10   Thoroughly clean each component part and place it on a clean work surface. Lightly lubricate the oil seal and O-ring(s) with clean fork oil.
11   Reassembly is a reversal of the dismantling procedure. Use a suitable length of metal tube to drift the bush and oil seal into position. The tube end making contact with the component must be square to the stanchion, properly chamfered and free of burrs.
12   Check the leg for correct operation before replenishing it with the correct quantity of specified oil.

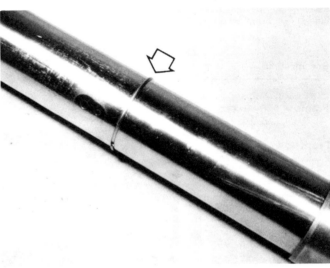

3.11a Check the fork stanchion circlip ...

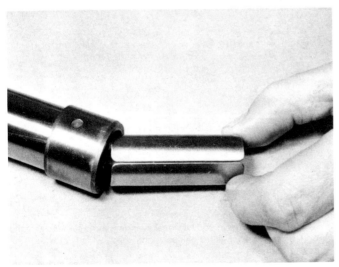

3.11b ... fit the spacer ...

3.11c ... align and fit the flat-sided washer ...

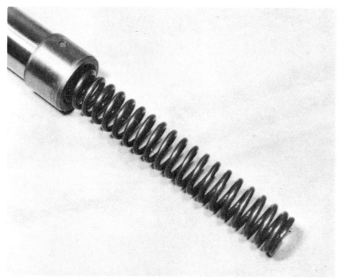

3.11d ... insert the fork spring into the stanchion (MX type)

3.11e Push the stanchion with bush into the lower leg ...

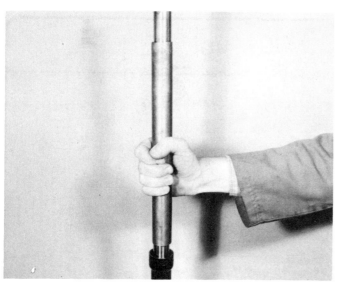

3.11f ... drift the bush into position ...

3.11g ... fit the oil seal and washer ...

3.11h ... fit the seal retaining clip (MX type)

3.11i Protect the stanchion by fitting a fork gaiter

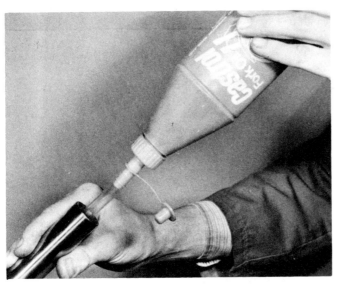

3.12a Replenish the fork leg with oil ...

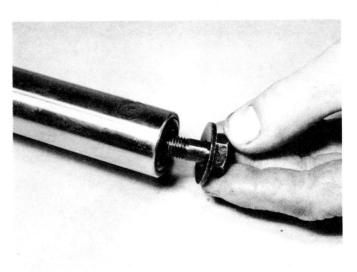

3.12b ... fit a serviceable O-ring and the top bolt with washer

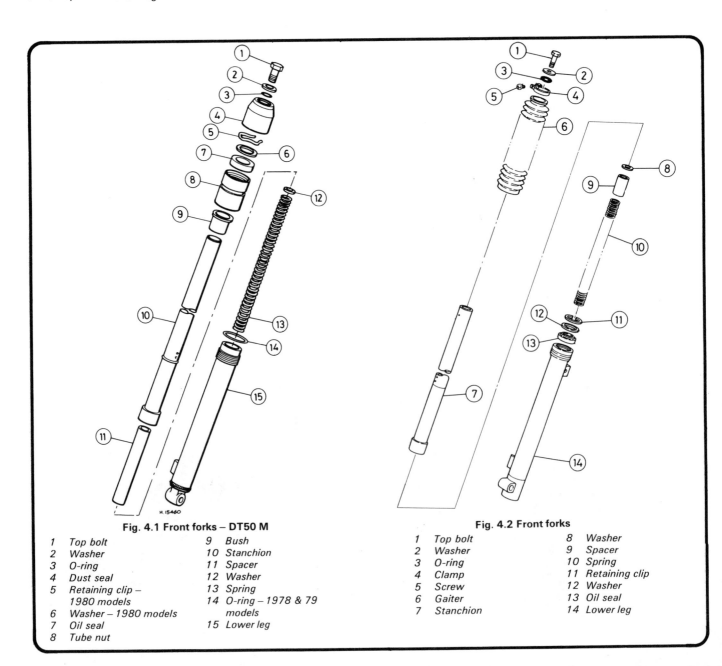

**Fig. 4.1 Front forks – DT50 M**

| | | | |
|---|---|---|---|
| 1 | Top bolt | 9 | Bush |
| 2 | Washer | 10 | Stanchion |
| 3 | O-ring | 11 | Spacer |
| 4 | Dust seal | 12 | Washer |
| 5 | Retaining clip – | 13 | Spring |
| | 1980 models | 14 | O-ring – 1978 & 79 |
| 6 | Washer – 1980 models | | models |
| 7 | Oil seal | 15 | Lower leg |
| 8 | Tube nut | | |

**Fig. 4.2 Front forks**

| | | | |
|---|---|---|---|
| 1 | Top bolt | 8 | Washer |
| 2 | Washer | 9 | Spacer |
| 3 | O-ring | 10 | Spring |
| 4 | Clamp | 11 | Retaining clip |
| 5 | Screw | 12 | Washer |
| 6 | Gaiter | 13 | Oil seal |
| 7 | Stanchion | 14 | Lower leg |

## 4 Steering head assembly: removal and refitting

1 Refer to Chapter 5 and remove the front wheel.
2 Refer to Section 2 and remove the front fork legs.
3 Unbolt the mudguard from the lower yoke. Isolate the battery by disconnecting one of its leads; this will prevent shorting of exposed contacts when disconnecting headstock components.
4 Use a commonsense approach when detaching components from the headstock. Remove only those components necessary to permit detachment of the upper and lower yokes; these should include the headlamp (and nacelle where fitted), instrument console and handlebars. Note the fitted position of the bars, protect the tank with rag and rest the bars on it.
5 Remove the steering stem top bolt through the upper yoke. Using a soft-faced hammer, gently tap the yoke upwards to free it.
6 Support the lower yoke. Using a C-spanner, remove the bearing adjuster ring. Make provision to catch any bolts that may fall from the bearings, remove the dust excluder and cone of the upper bearing and lower the yoke and stem from position.
7 Refer to the following Section for bearing examination and renovation.
8 When fitting the assembly, retain the balls around the lower cone with grease of the recommended type and fill both bearing cups with grease. Tighten the adjuster ring finger-tight.
9 Check all electrical leads and control cables are correctly routed. Refer to the specified torque settings. Check the headlamp beam height, see Chapter 6, and refer to Routine Maintenance for steering head bearing adjustment. Check all controls and instruments are functioning correctly.

## 5 Steering head bearings: examination and renovation

1 The bearing cup and cone tracks should be free from indentations or cracks. If necessary, renew the cups and cones as complete sets.
2 If any one ball is cracked or blemished, renew the complete set. Do not risk refitting defective balls, they are relatively cheap. There are nineteen balls in the lower race and twenty-two in the upper; this leaves a gap between any two balls which must not be filled otherwise wear will occur.
3 Drift each bearing cup from the steering head if necessary, using a long drift passed through the opposite end of the head. Ensure the cup leaves its location squarely by moving the drift around it.
4 The lower cone can be drifted off the steering stem with a flat chisel, keeping it square to the stem.
5 Before fitting new cups, clean and lightly grease their locations. Support the steering head as a wooden block whilst drifting each cup home. Using a short length of metal tube of the same outer diameter as the cup with a piece of wood placed across it will provide the most effective method of driving the cup squarely home. The tube ends must be square to its length. Clean and grease the stem before fitting the lower cone.

## 6 Fork yokes: examination

1 Renew any yoke which is damaged or cracked. Check for distortion by pushing the fork stanchions through the lower yoke and fitting the top yoke. If alignment is correct, the yokes are not bent.

## 7 Steering lock: renewal

1 Once operated, the lock prevents the handlebars from turning once they are set on full lock. If the lock malfunctions it must be renewed, repair is impracticable.
2 Some dismantling of the steering head will be necessary to allow removal of the lock securing screws or rivet. Obtain a key with the new lock and carry it when riding the machine.

## 8 Speedometer head and drive: examination and renovation

1 If the instrument fails to function, check the cable for breakage. A dry cable or one which is trapped or kinked will cause the instrument needle to jerk. Refer to Routine Maintenance for cable care. Refer to Chapter 5 for details of the drive gearbox.
2 It is not practicable to repair the instrument head; obtain a serviceable item. A speedometer in correct working order is required by law.
3 To remove the instrument, disconnect the drive cable by unscrewing its retaining ring, detach the instrument from its mounting bracket and unplug the bulb holders from its base.

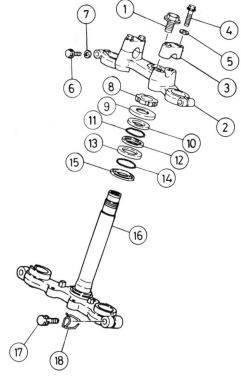

**Fig. 4.3 Steering head assembly**

| | | | |
|---|---|---|---|
| 1 | Top bolt | 10 | Upper bearing cone |
| 2 | Upper yoke | 11 | Bearing balls |
| 3 | Handlebar clamp – 2 off | 12 | Upper bearing cup |
| 4 | Bolt – 4 off | 13 | Lower bearing cup |
| 5 | Washer – 4 off | 14 | Bearing balls |
| 6 | Bolt – 2 off | 15 | Lower bearing cone |
| 7 | Washer – 2 off | 16 | Lower yoke |
| 8 | Adjusting nut | 17 | Bolt – 2 off |
| 9 | Dust cover | 18 | Cable guide |

8.3a Disconnect the speedometer drive cable ...

8.3b ... and detach the instrument from its mounting bracket (MX shown)

## 9  Swinging arm: removal, examination, renovation and refitting

1  Wear in the arm pivot bearings will cause imprecise handling with a tendency for the rear of the machine to twitch or hop. Support the machine with its rear wheel clear of the ground. Hold onto the main frame and pull and push the rear of the arm; play in the bearings will be magnified by the leverage effect produced.

2  Wear will necessitate bearing renewal. Refer to Chapter 5 and remove the rear wheel. Move the drive chain clear of the arm.

3  On DT50 M models, remove each suspension unit to arm securing nut, pull each unit off its stud and swing the arm down.

4  On MX models, remove the suspension unit to frame securing pin and lower the arm.

5  Remove the pivot shaft retaining nut (with spring washer, MX models) and use a soft-metal drift and hammer to displace the shaft. Manoeuvre the arm rearwards to clear the machine.

6  Thoroughly clean the arm and pivot components. Renew the nylon buffer of the left-hand bearing housing if it is excessively worn.

7  Renew the pivot shaft if its shank is stepped, badly scored or bent. No wear should exist between the shaft, pivot bearings and frame lugs. Obtain specialist advice when renovating the frame.

8  When removing worn bearings, refer to the accompanying figure and fabricate a puller. Do not risk damaging the bearing housings by attempting to drive the bearings out. If unsuccessful, return the arms to a Yamaha agent.

9  Lubricate each new bearing outer sleeve to aid fitting. Pull or drift each bearing home square to its housing.

10  Examine the arm for distortion and cracking. If repair is expensive, look around for a good secondhand item. Remove corrosion with a wire brush and derusting agents and replace the paint finish.

11  Align the arm in the frame. Lightly grease and fit the pivot shaft. On MX models, fit a serviceable spring washer. Tighten the shaft nut to the specified torque loading.

12  Check that the arm pivots smoothly before reconnecting the suspension unit(s). On DT50 M models tighten the unit securing nuts to the specified torque loading. On MX models, lightly grease the unit securing pin and washer, using a new split-pin to secure them.

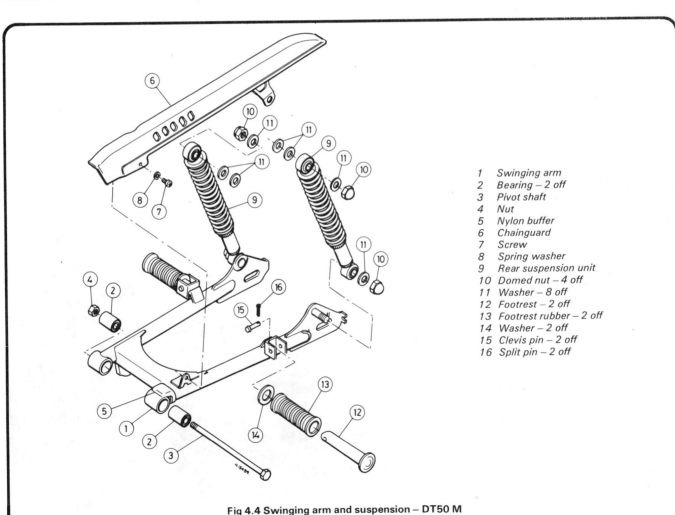

1   Swinging arm
2   Bearing – 2 off
3   Pivot shaft
4   Nut
5   Nylon buffer
6   Chainguard
7   Screw
8   Spring washer
9   Rear suspension unit
10  Domed nut – 4 off
11  Washer – 8 off
12  Footrest – 2 off
13  Footrest rubber – 2 off
14  Washer – 2 off
15  Clevis pin – 2 off
16  Split pin – 2 off

Fig 4.4 Swinging arm and suspension – DT50 M

9.11a Align the swinging arm in the frame ...

9.11b ... torque load the pivot shaft nut ...

9.12 ... and use a new split-pin to secure the suspension unit (MX shown)

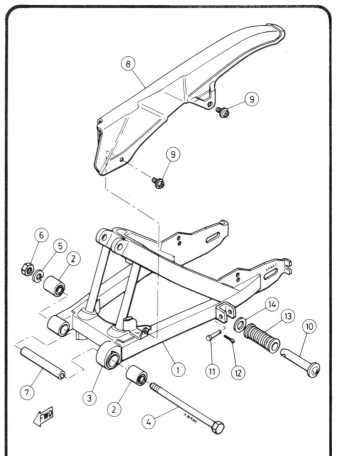

**Fig. 4.5 Swinging arm – MX models**

| | | | |
|---|---|---|---|
| 1 | Swinging arm | 8 | Chainguard |
| 2 | Bearing – 2 off | 9 | Screw – 2 off |
| 3 | Nylon buffer | 10 | Footrest – 2 off |
| 4 | Pivot shaft | 11 | Clevis pin – 2 off |
| 5 | Spring washer | 12 | Split pin – 2 off |
| 6 | Nut | 13 | Footrest rubber – 2 off |
| 7 | Spacer | 14 | Washer – 2 off |

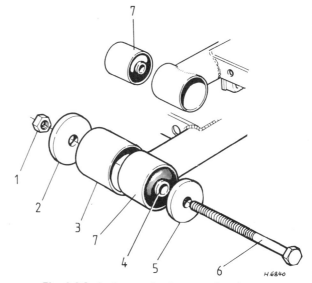

**Fig. 4.6 Swinging arm bush removal tool**

| | | | |
|---|---|---|---|
| 1 | Nut | 5 | Washer |
| 2 | Washer | 6 | Bolt |
| 3 | Tube | 7 | Bush |
| 4 | Swinging arm | | |

## 10 Rear suspension unit(s): examination and refitting

### DT50 M

1 Each unit is sealed; leakage, failure of damping, damage to the piston housing, a bent or corroded damper rod or deterioration of its rubber mounting bushes will necessitate renewal. Renew the units as a matched pair otherwise roadholding will suffer.

2 To prevent the back end collapsing, remove the units one at a time. Remove the retaining nuts and washers and pull each unit off its mounting studs.

3 If necessary, thoroughly clean each unit before fitting. Do not grease the damper rod, this will cause seal failure. Correctly position each washer and tighten each nut to the recommended torque loading.

### DT50 MX and 80 MX

4 If the unit is suspect, refer to Chapter 5 and remove the rear wheel. Refer to Chapter 2 and remove the fuel tank.

5 Remove the unit to frame securing pin, allow the swinging arm to drop and release the unit from the arm. Withdraw the unit.

6 Any of the faults mentioned in paragraph 1 will necessitate unit renewal. Although the spring can be removed for free length measurement, this will require special tools. Yamaha do not supply the spring as a separate item.

7 The unit contains highly compressed nitrogen gas, observe the following precautions

    a)    Do not deform the unit. This will result in poor damping.

    b)    Do not attempt to open or tamper with the unit. Serious injury may result.

    c)    Do not subject the unit to a high heat source. It will explode.

8 Do not just throw the unit away, return it to a Yamaha agent for proper disposal. Gas pressure must be released by drilling a hole in the gas chamber whilst wearing proper eye protection. Refer to the accompanying figure.

9 If necessary, thoroughly clean the unit before fitting. Lightly grease its securing pins and washers and fit new split-pins.

## 11 Frame: examination and renovation

1 If the frame is bent through accident damage, replacement is the most satisfactory solution; look around for a good secondhand item. Rejigging is possible but is a specialist task and can be expensive.

2 Clean the frame regularly, checking the welded joints for cracking. Minor damage can be repaired by welding or brazing. Remove corrosion with a wire brush and derusting agents, it can cause reduction in the material thickness.

3 A misaligned frame will cause handling problems and may promote 'speed wobbles'. If necessary, strip the machine completely and have the frame checked.

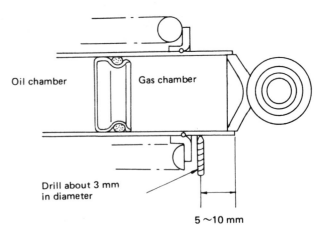

Fig. 4.7 Releasing rear suspension unit gas pressure – MX models

## 12 Footrests, prop stand and brake pedal: general maintenance

1 Frequently examine and lubricate each component; failure or incorrect operation can cause a serious accident. Check for free movement over the full operating range. Renew worn pivot components and fatigued or badly corroded springs. Check for security; split-pins must be correctly fitted.

2 If a component is bent, remove it and clamp it in a vice. Using a blow lamp or welding torch, heat the area around the bend to a cherry red. Carefully straighten the component by tapping it with a hammer.

3 Straightening a component with the metal cold will cause stress fractures, leading to fatigue. Before refitting the component, check for signs of failure and renew if in doubt.

# Chapter 5 Wheels, brakes and tyres

## Contents

## Specifications

### Brakes (front and rear)

| | |
|---|---|
| Type ............... | Internally expanding, single leading shoe, drum |
| Shoe lining thickness ............... | 4.0 mm (0.16 in) |
| Service limit ............... | 2.0 mm (0.08 in) |
| Drum internal diameter ............... | 110 mm (4.33 in) |
| Service limit ............... | 111 mm (4.37 in) |
| Return spring free length: | |
| DT50 M ............... | N/Av |
| DT50 MX and 80 MX ............... | 34.5 mm (1.36 in) |

### Wheels

| | DT50 M | DT50 MX and 80 MX |
|---|---|---|
| Type ............... | Conventional, steel-spoked with chromed steel rim | |
| Rim size: | | |
| Front ............... | 19 x 1.60 | 21 x 1.60 |
| Rear ............... | 17 x 1.60 | 18 x 1.60 |
| Rim runout (max) ............... | 2.0 mm (0.08 in) | 2.0 mm (0.08 in) |

### Tyres

| | DT50 M | DT50 MX and 80 MX |
|---|---|---|
| Size: | | |
| Front ............... | 2.50 – 19 4PR | 2.50 – 21 4PR |
| Rear ............... | 3.00 – 17 4PR | 3.00 – 18 4PR |
| Pressures: | | |
| Front ............... | 14.2 psi | 21 psi |
| Rear ............... | 17.1 psi | 26 psi |

### Final drive chain

| | DT50 M | DT50 MX and 80 MX |
|---|---|---|
| Make ............... | 101 | 010 |
| Type ............... | DK420 | DK420 |
| No of links ............... | 103 + link | 109 + link (50 MX) |
| | | 107 + link (80 MX) |
| Play ............... | 20 – 25 mm | 30 mm |
| | (0.8 – 1.0 in) | (1.2 in) |

### Torque wrench settings – kgf m (lbf ft)

| | DT50 M | DT50 MX and 80 MX |
|---|---|---|
| Front wheel spindle nut ............... | 3.0 (21.7) | 4.5 (32.5) |
| Rear wheel spindle nut ............... | 6.0 (43.3) | 60 (43.3) |
| Rear torque arm nuts ............... | 1.8 (13.0) | 1.8 (13.0) |
| Sprocket retaining nuts ............... | 2.5 (18.0) | 2.5 (18.0) |

## 1 General description

Each wheel comprises a chromed steel rim laced to an aluminium alloy hub by steel spokes. Refer to Specifications for wheel and tyre sizes. The tubed tyres have a block pattern tread suitable for both on- and off-road use. Each brake is drum with single leading shoe operation.

## 2 Wheels: examination and renovation

1 Refer to Routine Maintenance for details of this operation.

### 3  Front wheel: removal and refitting

1   Position a stout wooden crate or blocks beneath the engine so that the machine is well supported with the front wheel clear of the ground.
2   Pull the split-pin from the wheel spindle retaining nut. Remove the nut. Unclip the speedometer cable from the wheel hub and pull it clear. Detach the brake cable from the operating arm and brake backplate.
3   Support the wheel and pull the spindle clear. If necessary, use a soft-metal drift and hammer to tap it from position. Remove the wheel, noting the fitted position of washers and spacers.
4   Refer to the accompanying figure and check all spacers are correctly fitted before lifting the wheel into position. Ensure the fork leg spigot engages in the backplate slot otherwise the wheel will lock directly the brake is applied, with disastrous consequences.
5   Grease the spindle before insertion and tap it lightly to seat it. Tighten the retaining nut to the specified torque loading and fit a new split-pin.
6   Reconnect the speedometer and brake cables. Refer to Routine Maintenance and adjust the brake. Recheck all disturbed connections for security before taking the machine on the road.

3.4 Engage the fork leg spigot in the brake backplate slot

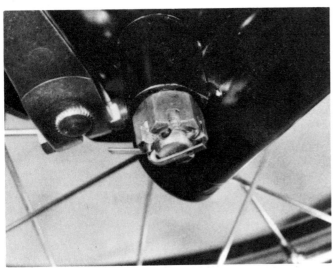

3.5 Lock the wheel spindle nut with a new split-pin

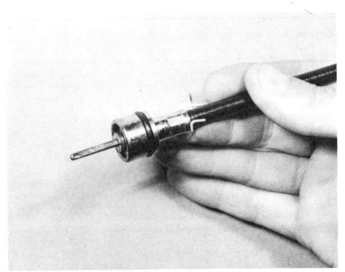

3.6a Examine the speedometer cable O-ring ...

3.6b ... retain the drive cable with the spring clip

3.6c Examine the brake cable return spring and gaiter ...

**Tyre removal:** Deflate inner tube and insert lever in close proximity to tyre valve

Use two levers to work bead over the edge of rim

When first bead is clear, remove tyre as shown

**Tyre fitting:** Inflate inner tube and insert in tyre

Lay tyre on rim and feed valve through hole in rim

Work first bead over rim, using lever in final section

Use similar technique for second bead, finish at tyre valve position

Push valve and tube up into tyre when fitting final section, to avoid trapping

3.6d ... and reconnect the brake cable (MX shown)

**Fig. 5.1 Front wheel – DT50 M**

| | | | |
|---|---|---|---|
| 1 | Hub | 18 | Cam shaft |
| 2 | Spoke | 19 | Brake shoe – 2 off |
| 3 | Rim | 20 | Return spring – 2 off |
| 4 | Tyre | 21 | Cam operating arm |
| 5 | Inner tube | 22 | Bolt |
| 6 | Rim tape | 23 | Nut |
| 7 | Centre spacer | 24 | Washer |
| 8 | Spacer flange | 25 | Speedometer driven gear |
| 9 | Bearing – 2 off | 26 | Bush |
| 10 | Oil seal | 27 | Oil seal |
| 11 | Oil seal | 28 | O-ring |
| 12 | Circlip | 29 | Retaining clip |
| 13 | Washer – 2 off | 30 | Wheel spindle |
| 14 | Drive plate | 31 | Spacer |
| 15 | Drive gear | 32 | Retaining nut |
| 16 | Brake backplate | 33 | Split pin |
| 17 | Plug | 34 | Washer |

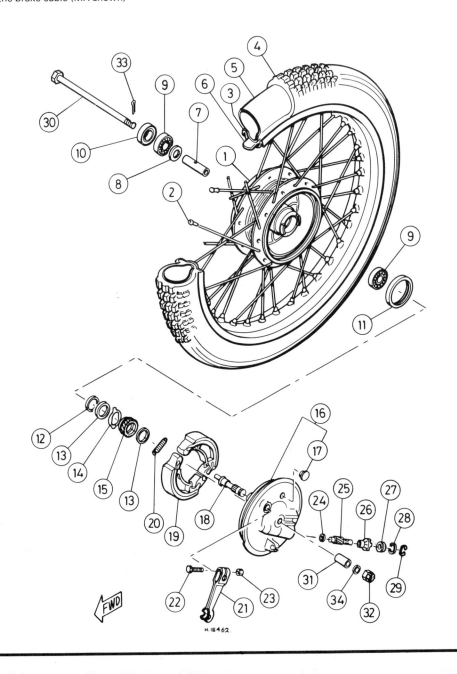

H.15462

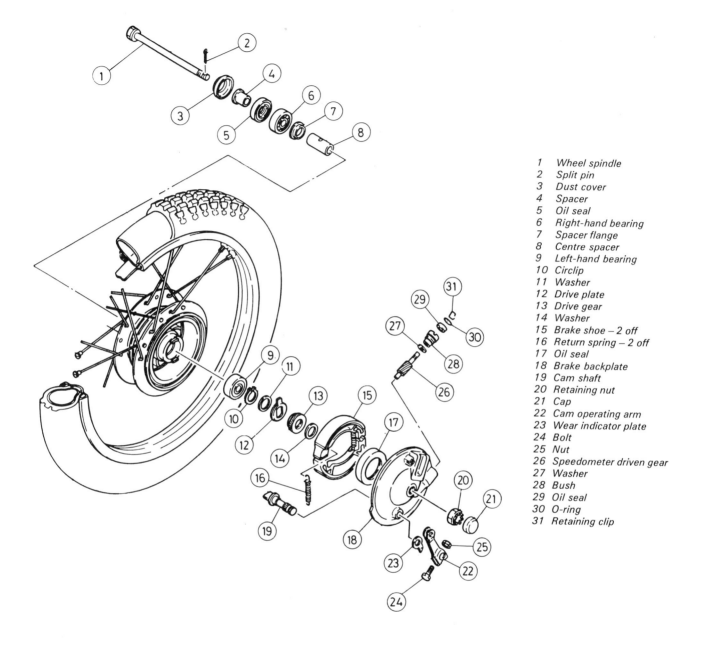

1   Wheel spindle
2   Split pin
3   Dust cover
4   Spacer
5   Oil seal
6   Right-hand bearing
7   Spacer flange
8   Centre spacer
9   Left-hand bearing
10  Circlip
11  Washer
12  Drive plate
13  Drive gear
14  Washer
15  Brake shoe − 2 off
16  Return spring − 2 off
17  Oil seal
18  Brake backplate
19  Cam shaft
20  Retaining nut
21  Cap
22  Cam operating arm
23  Wear indicator plate
24  Bolt
25  Nut
26  Speedometer driven gear
27  Washer
28  Bush
29  Oil seal
30  O-ring
31  Retaining clip

Fig. 5.2 Front wheel − MX models

## 4   Rear wheel: removal and refitting

Position a stout wooden crate or blocks beneath the engine so that the machine is well supported with the rear wheel clear of the ground.
2   Pull the split-pin from the wheel spindle retaining nut. Remove the nut. Remove the split-pin, nut and spring washer which retain the torque arm to the brake backplate. Detach the arm.
3   Remove the nut from the brake rod end. Depress the brake pedal so the rod leaves the trunnion of the operating arm. Retain the nut, trunnion, spring and washer (DT50 M only) to prevent loss.
4   Lay a length of clean rag beneath the final drive chain. Rotate the wheel to align the chain split link with the wheel sprocket. Using flat-nose pliers, remove the spring clip from the link. Remove the link, lift the chain ends off the sprocket and place them on the rag.

5   Support the wheel and pull out the spindle. If necessary, use a soft-metal drift and hammer to tap it from position. Remove the wheel, noting the fitted position of washers and spacers.
6   Refer to the accompanying figure and check all spacers are correctly fitted before lifting the wheel into position. Grease the spindle before insertion and tap it lightly to seat it. Fit the retaining nut, finger-tight.
7   Reconnect the brake rod and torque arm. Renew the arm retaining washer if flattened, tighten the nut to the specified torque loading and fit a new split-pin.
8   Reconnect and adjust the chain, see Routine Maintenance. Note instructions for fitting of the split link and spindle retaining nut.
9   Refer to Routine Maintenance and adjust the brake. Recheck all disturbed connections for security before taking the machine on the road.

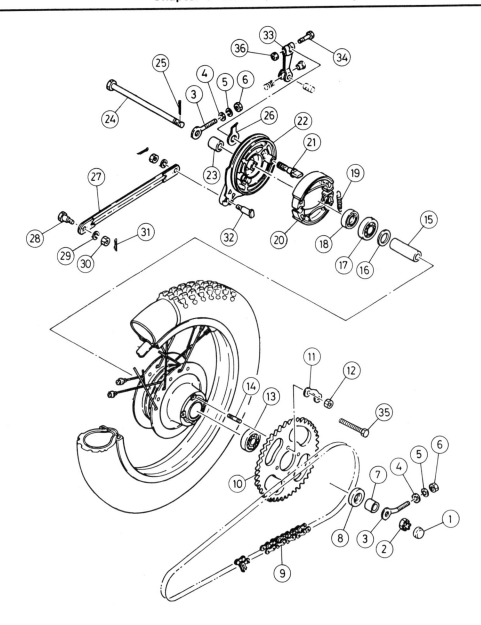

**Fig. 5.3 Rear wheel**

| | |
|---|---|
| 1 | Cap |
| 2 | Retaining nut |
| 3 | Chain adjuster – 2 off |
| 4 | Washer – 2 off |
| 5 | Spring washer – 2 off |
| 6 | Nut – 2 off |
| 7 | Left-hand spacer |
| 8 | Oil seal |
| 9 | Final drive chain |
| 10 | Sprocket |
| 11 | Tab washer – 2 off |
| 12 | Nut – 4 off |
| 13 | Left-hand bearing |
| 14 | Stud – 4 off (MX models) |
| 15 | Centre spacer |
| 16 | Spacer flange |
| 17 | Right-hand spacer |
| 18 | Oil seal |
| 19 | Spring – 2 off |
| 20 | Brake shoe – 2 off |
| 21 | Brake camshaft |
| 22 | Brake backplate |
| 23 | Right-hand spacer |
| 24 | Wheel spindle |
| 25 | Split pin |
| 26 | Wear indicator plate |
| 27 | Torque arm |
| 28 | Bolt |
| 29 | Spring washer |
| 30 | Nut – 2 off |
| 31 | Split pin – 2 off |
| 32 | Bolt |
| 33 | Brake operating arm |
| 34 | Bolt |
| 35 | Bolt – 4 off (DT50 M) |
| 36 | Nut |

## 5  Wheel bearings: removal, examination and refitting

1  Remove the wheel and detach the brake backplate. Support the wheel hub on wooden blocks placed as close to the bearing as possible.

2  Place the end of a long drift against the upper face of the lower bearing, moving the centre spacer sideways. Tap the bearing downwards, moving the drift around the bearing so that it leaves the hub squarely.

3  Any oil seal will be removed with the bearing and should be renewed as a matter of course. Withdraw the spacer, invert the wheel and drift out the second bearing.

4  Use petrol to clean all grease from the hub and bearings. Observe the necessary fire precautions. Spin each bearing and check for play or roughness. Renew if in doubt.

5  Before fitting, pack each bearing with the recommended grease. Clean and lightly grease each bearing housing. Check the housings for abnormal wear caused by movement of the bearing outer race. Obtain specialist advice if a bearing is a loose fit in the hub.

6  Where applicable, fit the bearing with its sealed side facing outboard. Select a socket which has an overlap diameter slightly less than the bearing outer race. Support the hub and use the socket and a soft-faced hammer to drift the first bearing into its housing. Keep the bearing square to the hub otherwise the housing surface may be broached.

7   Invert the wheel and insert the spacer. Pack the hub no more than $\frac{2}{3}$ full with fresh grease. Fit the second bearing . Use the socket and hammer to tap home each new seal. Lightly grease the seal lip.

## 6   Speedometer drive gear: examination and renovation

1   Remove the front wheel and detach the brake backplate; the drive gear is fitted in the backplate.
2   Remove the circlip to release the plate washer, drive plate, drive gear and second washer. Clean each part and the worm gear in the backplate. Do not remove the worm gear unless damaged; this is difficult to achieve.
3   Badly worn drive plate tangs are the normal cause of drive failure. Renew any part which is obviously worn.
4   Failure of the large oil seal which surrounds the drive gear will allow grease from the gear to contaminate the brake linings. If defective, carefully lever the seal from position with a screwdriver, taking care not to damage the backplate. Check the new seal enters its location squarely. Start with finger pressure then place a strip of wood across it, tapping down on the wood to drive the seal home.
5   Lightly grease each part of the drive before fitting. Check the drive plate turns smoothly, align it with the wheel hub and grease the seal lip before fitting the backplate.

5.6 Fit each wheel bearing with its sealed side outboard ...

5.7a ... fit the bearing spacer ...

5.7b ... and fit the second bearing

5.7c Lightly grease the seal lip

6.4 Remove the speedometer drive gear seal, if defective

6.5a Fit the drive gear plate washer ...

6.5b ... mesh the worm and drive gears ...

6.5c ... retain the drive plate and washer with the circlip

7.2 Lock the sprocket retaining nuts with the tab washers

## 7 Wheel sprocket: examination and renewal

1    Renew the sprocket if its teeth are hooked or badly worn. It is bad practice to renew the sprocket on its own; both drive sprockets should be renewed, preferably with the chain. Running old and new parts together will result in rapid wear.

2    Remove the wheel and bend back the locking tab from each sprocket securing nut (or bolt). Remove the nuts, tab washers and sprocket. When fitting, do not rebend the locking tabs, renew the washers if necessary. Tighten the nuts evenly and in a diagonal sequence to the specified torque setting.

## 8 Final drive chain: examination, adjustment and lubrication

1    Refer to Routine Maintenance for details of this operation.

## 9 Brakes: adjustment and wear check

1    Refer to Routine Maintenance for details of these operations.

## 10 Brakes: examination, renovation and reassembly

1    It is false economy to cut corners with brake components; the safety of machine and rider depends on their good condition.

2    Remove the wheel and pull the brake backplate from the hub. If the brake linings are contaminated by oil or grease or they have worn beyond the specified limit, renew the shoes.

3    Remove surface dirt with a petrol-soaked rag. The dirt contains asbestos and is harmful if inhaled. Ease down high spots with a file. There is no satisfactory method of degreasing the linings.

4    If necessary, remove the shoes by folding them together into a 'V' and pulling them off the backplate. Detach the springs and examine them for fatigue or failure. Refer to Specifications and measure the spring free length; alternatively, compare with a new item to check the springs have not stretched.

5    Remove the cam operating arm, marking its fitted position. Withdraw the cam and clean and grease its shaft. Refit the cam, the wear indicator (where fitted) and the pivot stud with brake grease.

6    Before refitting existing shoes, break the surface glaze with glasspaper. Do not inhale any dust. Assemble the springs and shoes

and reverse the removal procedure to fit them to the backplate. Do not risk distortion by using excessive force.

7   Examine the drum surface for scoring, oil contamination or wear beyond the service limit, all of which will impair braking efficiency. Remove dust with a petrol-soaked rag; the dust is harmful if inhaled. Use a rag soaked in petrol to remove oil deposits; observe the necessary fire precautions.

8   If the drum is deeply scored, it must be skimmed on a lathe or renewed. Excessive skimming will adversely affect brake performance; consult a specialist.

## 11  Valve cores and caps

1   Dirt under the valve seat will cause a puzzling 'slow-puncture'. Check for leaks by applying spittle to the valve and watching for bubbles.

2   The cap is a safety device and should always be fitted. It keeps dirt out of the valve and provides a second seal in case of valve failure, thus preventing an accident resulting from sudden deflation.

10.5a Fit the brake cam ...

10.5b ... align the wear indicator pointer over the splines (MX only) ...

10.5c ... and fit the cam operating arm

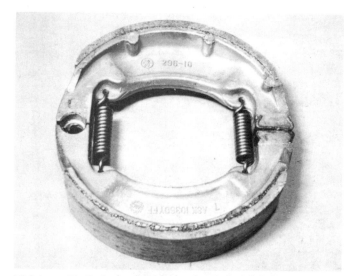

10.6 Assemble the brake shoes and springs before fitting

## 12  Tyres: removal, repair and refitting

1   Remove the wheel and deflate the tyre by removing the valve core. Push the tyre bead on both sides away from the wheel rim and into its centre well. Remove the locking ring and push the valve into the tyre.

2   Insert a tyre lever close to the valve and lever the tyre bead over the outside of the rim. Work around the rim until one side of the tyre is completely free. No great force is required; if resistance is encountered check both beads have fully entered the rim well. Remove the inner tube.

3   Work from the other side of the wheel and ease the other bead over the outside of the rim furthest away until the tyre is free.

4   If the tube is punctured, inflate it and immerse in water. Bubbles will indicate the source of the leak which should be marked. Deflate and dry the tube. Clean the punctured area with a petrol soaked rag. When dry, apply rubber solution. With the solution dry, remove the patch backing and apply the patch.

5   Self vulcanizing patches are the best type. It may be necessary to remove a protective covering from the top of the patch after application. Synthetic rubber tubes may require a special patch and adhesive.

6    If the tube is already patched or if it is torn, renew it. Sudden deflation can cause an accident.

7    Before fitting the tyre, check its inside and outside for the cause of the puncture. Do not fit a tyre with damaged tread or sidewalls. The rim tape must be fitted, this prevents the spoke ends chafing the tube and causing punctures. Fitting can be aided by dusting the tyre beads with french chalk. Washing up liquid can be used but may cause corrosion of the inner rim, use it sparingly to avoid tyre creep.

8    Inflate the tube just enough for it to assume a circular shaft, no more, and push it fully into the tyre. Lay the tyre on the rim at an angle. Insert the valve through the rim hole and screw the locking ring on the first few threads.

9    Starting at the point furthest from the valve, push the tyre bead over the rim and into the centre well. Work around the tyre until the whole of one side is on the rim. If necessary, use a tyre lever during the final stage.

10   Check there is no pull on the valve and repeat the procedure to fit the second bend into the rim. Finish adjacent to the valve, pushing it into the tyre as far as the locking ring will allow thus ensuring the tube is not trapped when the last section of bead is levered over the rim.

11   Check the tube is not trapped; reinflate it to the specified pressure and tighten the valve locking ring. Check the tyre is correctly seated on the rim. A thin rib moulded around each tyre wall should be equidistant from the rim at all points. If the tyre is uneven on the rim, try bouncing the wheel to reseat it. Fit the valve dust cap.

# Chapter 6 Electrical system

## Contents

## Specifications

### Battery

| | | |
|---|---|---|
| Type: | | |
| DT50 M | 6N4A – 4D | |
| DT50 MX and 80 MX | 6N4B – 2A – 3 | |
| Voltage | 6 volt | |
| Capacity | 4 Ah | |
| Electrolyte specific gravity | 1.26 at 20°C (68°F) | |
| Earth | Negative | |

### Fuse rating

10 amp

### Rectifier

| | |
|---|---|
| Make | Toshiba S5108 or Stanley DE4504 |
| Type | Single phase, half wave, silicon |
| Capacity | 4 amp |
| Voltage | 400 volt |

### Flywheel generator

| | DT50 M | DT50 MX and 80 MX |
|---|---|---|
| Charging coil resistance | 0.32 ohm ± 10% | 0.36 ohm ± 10% |
| Charging output: | | |
| Lights on | 0.15 – 0.40 amp at 8000 rpm | Above 0.8 amp at 3000 rpm<br>Below 2.0 amp at 8000 rpm |
| Lights off | Above 0.1 amp at 2000 rpm<br>Below 4.0 amp at 8000 rpm | Above 1.3 amp at 3000 rpm<br>Below 2.0 amp at 8000 rpm |
| Lighting coil resistance | 0.51 ohm ± 10% | 0.26 ohm ± 10% |
| Lighting output: | | |
| At 2500 rpm | Above 6.0 volt | Above 5.8 volt |
| At 8000 rpm | Below 8.5 volt | Below 8.5 volt |

### Bulbs

| | |
|---|---|
| Headlamp: | |
| DT50 M | 7V 18/18W |
| DT50 MX and 80 MX | 6V, 25/25W |
| Tail/stop lamp | 6V, 5/21W |
| Direction indicators: | |
| DT50 M and MX | 6V, 10W |
| DT80 MX | 6V, 15W |
| Pilot lamp – DT80 MX only | 6V, 3W |
| Speedometer light | 6V, 3W |
| Neutral indicator | 6V, 3W |
| Direction indicator warning light | 6V, 3W |
| Main beam indicator | 6V, 3W |

## 1 General description

The flywheel generator stator incorporates a coil to provide lighting and battery charging power and one to provide ignition source power.

The charging coil produces alternating current which is converted to direct current by a silicon diode rectifier to make it compatible with the battery and system components. The rectifier effectively blocks half of the output wave by acting as a one-way electronic switch; this system is known as half-wave rectification. Lighting is provided by a tap taken off the charging coil which feeds alternating current direct to the main lighting circuit. On DT50 MX and 80 MX models, a voltage regulator of the Zener diode type is incorporated in the system. This controls the charging voltage during daylight riding and, when the lights are switched on, controls voltage to the lights thus preventing bulb blowing due to voltage surge. On DT50 M models this problem was partially overcome by fitting a 7 volt headlamp bulb to a 6 volt system. In the event of a short circuit or sudden surge, the circuit is protected by a 10 amp fuse incorporated in the battery positive lead. The fuse forms a weak link which will blow and thus prevent damage to the circuit and components.

## 2 Testing the electrical system

1   Single continuity checks, used when testing switches, wiring and connections, can be carried out using a battery and bulb arrangement to provide a test circuit. For most tests however, a pocket multimeter should be considered essential.

2   A basic multimeter capable of measuring volts and ohms can be purchased for a reasonable sum and will prove invaluable. Separate volt and ohm meters can be used, provided those with correct operating ranges are available. If generator output is to be checked, an ammeter of 0-4 amperes range will be required.

3   Take care when performing any electrical test, some electrical components can be damaged if incorrectly connected or inadvertently earthed. Note instructions regarding meter probe connections.

4   If in doubt or where test equipment is not available, seek professional assistance. Do not risk damaging expensive electrical parts.

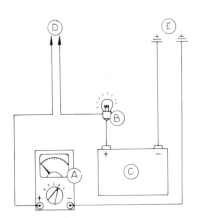

**Fig. 6.1 Simple testing arrangement for checking the electrical system**

| | | | |
|---|---|---|---|
| A | Multimeter | D | Positive probe |
| B | Bulb | E | Negative probe |
| C | Battery | | |

## 3 Wiring: layout and examination

1   The wiring is colour-coded, corresponding with the accompanying wiring diagram. Socket connectors are designed so that reconnection can only be made correctly.

2   Check for breaks or frayed outer coverings which will cause short circuits. A wire may become trapped, breaking the inner core but leaving the resilient outer cover thereby causing mysterious intermittent or total circuit failure. Corroded or badly made connections will also cause problems.

3   Intermittent short circuits can often be tracd to a chafed wire which passes through or close to a metal component. Avoid situations where a wire is tightly bent or can be trapped between moving parts.

## 4 Flywheel generator: output check

### Charging coil performance

1   Disconnect the positive (+) battery connections. Check both connection halves are clean and firmly connect an ammeter between them, setting it on its dc range. Start the engine. The meter readings should correspond with those given in Specifications.

### Lighting coil performance

2   Remove the headlamp reflector unit. Disconnect the yellow lead running from the headlamp bulb holder to the dip switch.

3   Set a multimeter on its 0-10 ac volt range and connect its positive probe to the lead terminal. Earth the meter negative probe. Switch the lighting to 'On' and start the engine. The meter readings should correspond with those given in Specifications.

### Continuity checks

4   If the results of the above tests prove unsatisfactory continue by making resistance tests of the coils. Refer to the accompanying wiring diagram and identify the lead running from the coil in question by the colour coding. Disconnect the generator from the main wiring loom.

5   Set a multimeter to its resistance function and measure for resistance across the coil windings. When connecting one meter probe to earth, select a clean, unprotected point on the crankcase. The meter reading should correspond with that given in Specifications of this Chapter (charging and lighting) or Chapter 3 (ignition source).

6   If the check is unsatisfactory, the coil is unserviceable and must be renewed. If it transpires that the coils are good, but poor charging or lighting performance is still experienced, continue with the tests in the next two Sections.

## 5 Rectifier : testing

1   The rectifier must be kept clean and dry and mounted so that it is not exposed to direct contamination by oil or water yet has free circulation of air to permit cooling. It can be damaged by inadvertently reversing the battery connections.

2   To test, set a multimeter to its resistance function (x1 ohm range) and connect its probes to the unit connectors. Note the meter reading and reverse the probes. If one reading shows continuity and the other non-continuity, the unit is serviceable.

## 6 Voltage regulator: testing – DT50 MX and 80 MX

1   The regulator can become damaged by poor earth connections or short circuiting in the system. Blowing bulbs or suddenly dimming lights will indicate unit failure.

2   Test by substitution, but first check lighting coil performance and eliminate all other possible causes of voltage output control faults.

## 7 Battery: examination and maintenance

1   Normal maintenance requires keeping the electrolyte level between the upper and lower marks on the battery case and checking the vent tube is correctly routed and not blocked. Unless acid is split, top up with distilled water.

2   If electrolyte level drops rapidly, suspect over charging or leakage. A cracked battery case cannot be effectively repaired and will necessitate battery renewal. Acid spillage must be neutralised with an alkali (washing soda or baking powder) and washed away with fresh water, otherwise serious corrosion will occur. Top up with sulphuric acid of 1.260 specific gravity.

3   Warpage of the plates and separators indicates an expiring battery as does sediment filling the gap between the case bottom and plates.

4   Check the lead connections are tight and free from corrosion. If

necessary, remove corrosion by scraping with a knife, finishing with emery cloth. Remake the connections and smear with petroleum jelly (not grease) to prevent further corrosion.

5    Recharging is required when the acid specific gravity falls below 1.260 (at 20°C – 68°F). Take the reading at the top of the meniscus with the hydrometer vertical. It is advisable to give the battery a 'refresher' charge every six weeks or so if the machine is rarely used. If left discharged for too long, the battery plates will sulphate and inhibit recharging. Refer to the following Section for charging procedure.

6    Take great care to protect the eyes and skin against accidental spillage of acid when holding the battery. Wear eyeshields at all times. Eyes contaminated with acid must be immediately flushed with fresh water and examined by a dealer. Similar attention should be given to a spillage on the skin.

## 8  Battery: charging

1    Battery life will be effectively shortened if charged at a rate exceeding about 0.8 amp. Charge in a well ventilated area, check the side vent is clear and remove the cell caps, otherwise the gas created within the battery might burst the case with disastrous consequences. Do not charge the battery in situ with its leads connected; this can damage the rectifier.

2    Check the charger connections are correct, red to positive (+), black negative (–). When refitting the battery, connect its black (negative) lead to earth otherwise the system will be permanently damaged.

3    Sulphuric acid is extremely corrosive. Wash hands promptly after handling the battery because its case is likely to be contaminated. Note the following precautions:

Do not allow smoking or naked flames near batteries.
Do avoid acid contact with skin, eyes and clothing.
Do keep battery electrolyte level maintained.
Do avoid over-high charge rates.
Do avoid leaving the battery discharged.
Do avoid freezing.
Do use only distilled or demineralised water for topping up.

## 9  Fuse: renewal

1    A plastic holder fitted to the battery positive lead contains the 10 amp fuse and its spare. Before replacing a blown fuse, check the system thoroughly to trace and eliminate the fault. If no spare is available, a 'get you home' remedy is to remove the fuse, wrap it in silver paper and refit it. Never do this if there is evidence of an electrical fault otherwise more serious damage will result. Replace the 'doctored' fuse at the earliest opportunity and carry a spare.

## 10  Bulbs: renewal

1    All bulbs on these machines are of the bayonet type and can be released by pushing in, turning anti-clockwise and pulling from the holder. The tail/stop lamp is fitted with a double filament bulb which has offset pins to prevent unintentional reversal in its holder.

2    Gain access to the main headlamp bulb holder by detaching the rim, complete with reflector and glass, from the shell or nacelle. Unclip the holder from the centre of the reflector to expose the bulb. DT80 MX models have a parking lamp fitted; pull the holder from the reflector to expose the bulb.

3    The tail/stop and direction indicator bulbs can be removed after detachment of the plastic lens, which will be secured by screws or clipped in position. Take care not to tear the lens seal (where fitted); this keeps moisture and dirt away from the backplate and electrical contacts and must be renewed if damaged.

4    The instrument and warning light bulbs are fitted in rubber holders which can be unplugged from the base of the instrument or console once it is exposed.

5    Clean any corrosion or moisture from the holder and check its contacts are free to move when depressed. Fit the bulb and lens. A lens can be cracked if its securing screws are overtightened. After tightening the headlamp rim, check beam alignment.

10.1a The headlamp rim is retained by a single screw (MX shown)

10.1b Remove the headlamp bulb holder from the reflector (MX shown)

10.2a Use a screwdriver to remove a lens which is clipped in position

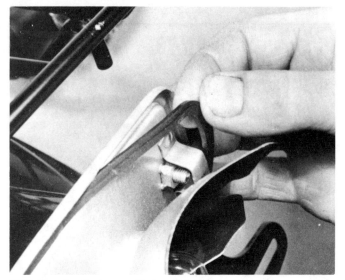

10.2b Examine the lens seal (where fitted)

10.3 The instrument bulbs are fitted in rubber holders

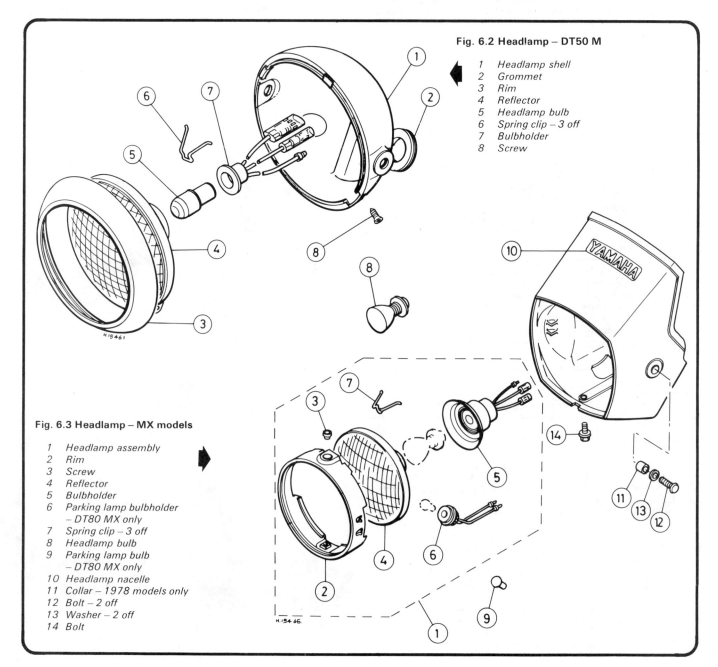

Fig. 6.2 Headlamp – DT50 M

1  Headlamp shell
2  Grommet
3  Rim
4  Reflector
5  Headlamp bulb
6  Spring clip – 3 off
7  Bulbholder
8  Screw

Fig. 6.3 Headlamp – MX models

1   Headlamp assembly
2   Rim
3   Screw
4   Reflector
5   Bulbholder
6   Parking lamp bulbholder
    – DT80 MX only
7   Spring clip – 3 off
8   Headlamp bulb
9   Parking lamp bulb
    – DT80 MX only
10  Headlamp nacelle
11  Collar – 1978 models only
12  Bolt – 2 off
13  Washer – 2 off
14  Bolt

## 11 Headlamp: beam alignment

1 UK regulations stipulate that the headlamp must be aligned so that the light will not dazzle a person standing at a distance greater than 25 feet from the lamp, whose eye level is not less than 3 feet 6 inches above that place. It is easy to approximate this setting by placing the machine 25 feet away from a wall, on a level road, and setting the dip beam height so that it is concentrated at the same height as the distance of the centre of the headlamp from the ground. The rider must be seated normally during this operation and also the pillion passenger, if one is carried regularly.

2 To effect beam vertical alignment, loosen the headlamp shell or nacelle securing screws and pivot the lamp up or down as required.

## 12 Switches: testing

1 Before suspecting a switch, refer to Section 2 and check its circuit wiring.

2 The ignition, neutral indicator and top lamp switches are all sealed and must be renewed if unserviceable. Dirty contacts are the cause of most troubles with handlebar switches; these can be cleaned with a special electrical contact cleaner. Internal breakage will necessitate switch renewal.

3 To test, refer to the accompanying wiring diagram and identify the switch and its circuit. Prevent the possibility of a short circuit by disconnecting the battery. Disconnect the switch, set a multimeter to its resistance function and check for continuity between the switch terminals (and earth, where necessary) whilst operating the switch. If no continuity is found in the positions shown for continuity in the diagram, the switch is defective.

4 It is dangerous to have a defective lighting switch whilst riding at night. Failure will plunge the rider into darkness with disastrous consequences.

## 13 Stop lamp switches: adjustment

1 The stop lamp is operated by two switches, front and rear. Only the rear switch is adjustable. If the lamp is late in operating, raise the switch body by turning its adjuster nut clockwise whilst holding the switch steady. If the lamp is permanently on, then lower its body. As a guide to operation, the lamp should illuminate immediately the brake pedal is depressed.

## 14 Flasher unit: renewal

1 If the unit is functioning correctly, a series of clicks will be heard when the indicator lamps are operating. If it malfunctions and the bulbs are serviceable, the usual symptom is one flash before the unit goes dead.

2 The unit is sealed; to renew it, unplug the electrical connector and slide the unit from its mounting. Do not subject the new unit to sudden shock, it is easily damaged. Fitting is a direct reversal of removal.

## 15 Horn: adjustment and renewal

1 Volume adjustment is provided by means of a screw at the rear of the horn case. Turn the screw fractionally to increase volume.

2 The unit is sealed; to renew it, disconnect the electrical wires from its terminals, having noted their fitted positions, and unbolt the unit from its mounting. Fitting is a direct reversal of removal.

11.2 Loosen the headlamp securing screws to effect beam alignment (MX shown)

13.1 Turn the stop lamp switch adjuster nut to effect operation

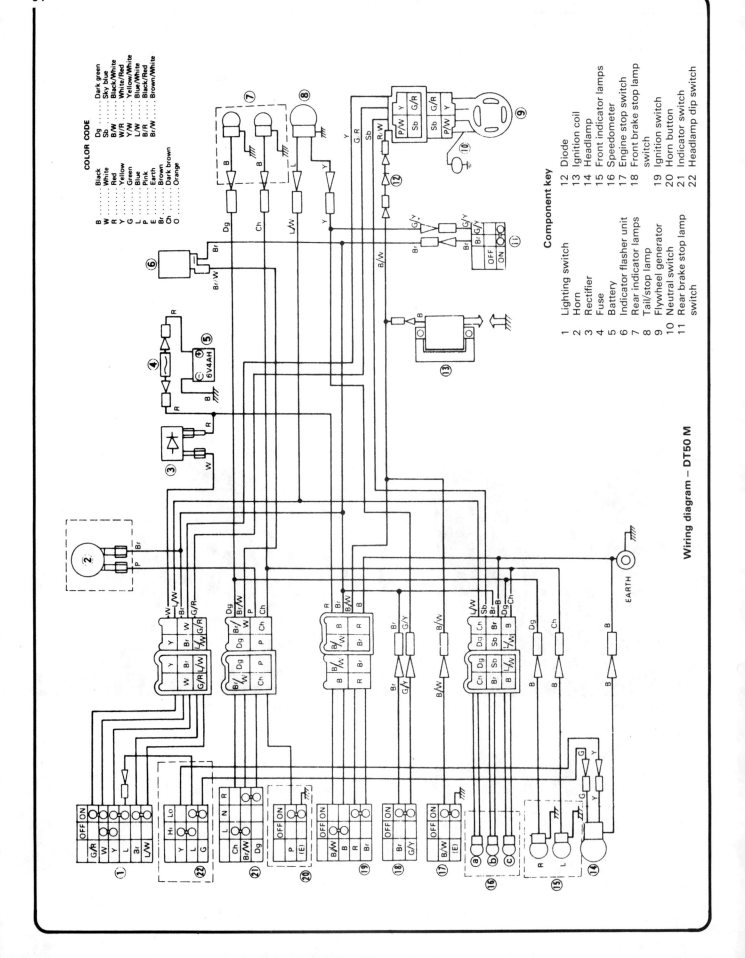

**COLOR CODE**

| | | | |
|---|---|---|---|
| B | Black | Dg | Dark green |
| W | White | Sb | Sky blue |
| R | Red | B/W | Black/White |
| Y | Yellow | W/R | White/Red |
| G | Green | Y/W | Yellow/White |
| L | Blue | L/W | Blue/White |
| P | Pink | B/R | Black/Red |
| E | Earth | Br/W | Brown/White |
| Br | Brown | | |
| Ch | Dark brown | | |
| O | Orange | | |

**Component key**

1　Lighting switch
2　Horn
3　Rectifier
4　Fuse
5　Battery
6　Indicator flasher unit
7　Rear indicator lamps
8　Tail/stop lamp
9　Flywheel generator
10　Neutral switch
11　Rear brake stop lamp switch
12　Diode
13　Ignition coil
14　Headlamp
15　Front indicator lamps
16　Speedometer
17　Engine stop switch
18　Front brake stop lamp switch
19　Ignition switch
20　Horn button
21　Indicator switch
22　Headlamp dip switch

**Wiring diagram – DT50 M**

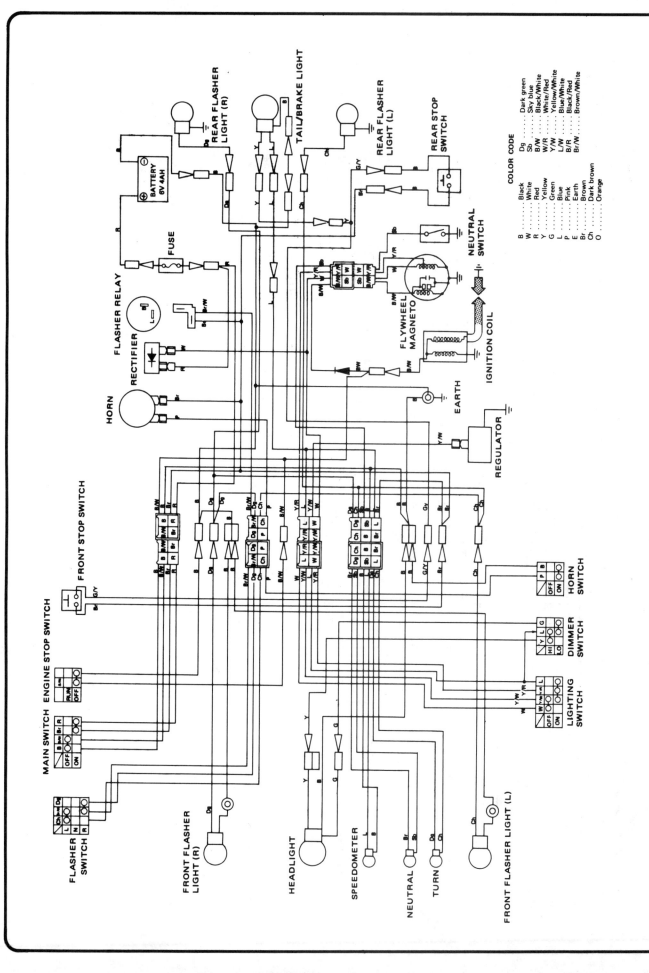

Wiring diagram – DT50 MX

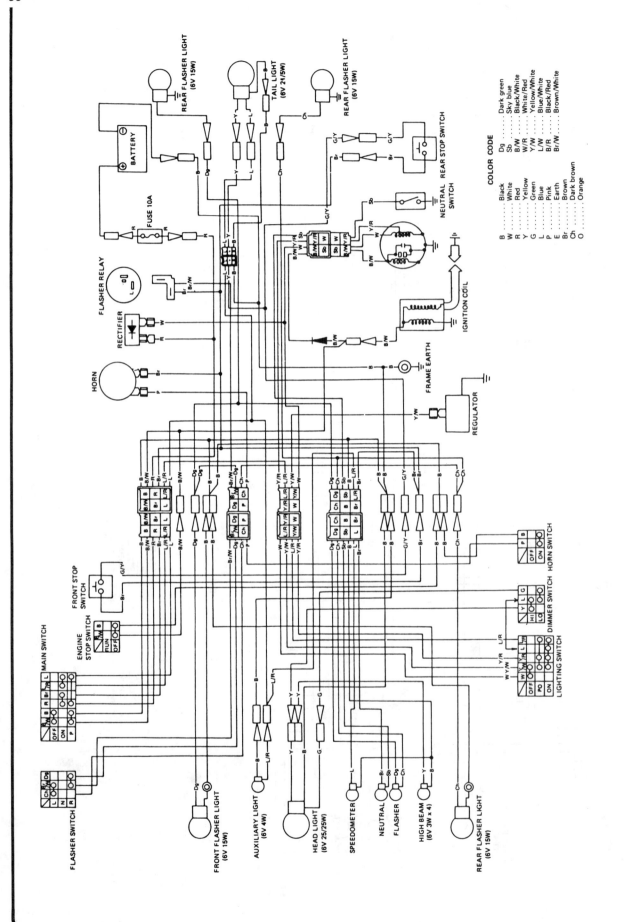

Wiring diagram – DT80 MX

# Conversion factors

### Length (distance)

| | | | | |
|---|---|---|---|---|
| Inches (in) | X 25.4 | = Millimetres (mm) | X 0.0394 | = Inches (in) |
| Feet (ft) | X 0.305 | = Metres (m) | X 3.281 | = Feet (ft) |
| Miles | X 1.609 | = Kilometres (km) | X 0.621 | = Miles |

### Volume (capacity)

| | | | | |
|---|---|---|---|---|
| Cubic inches (cu in; in$^3$) | X 16.387 | = Cubic centimetres (cc; cm$^3$) | X 0.061 | = Cubic inches (cu in; in$^3$) |
| Imperial pints (Imp pt) | X 0.568 | = Litres (l) | X 1.76 | = Imperial pints (Imp pt) |
| Imperial quarts (Imp qt) | X 1.137 | = Litres (l) | X 0.88 | = Imperial quarts (Imp qt) |
| Imperial quarts (Imp qt) | X 1.201 | = US quarts (US qt) | X 0.833 | = Imperial quarts (Imp qt) |
| US quarts (US qt) | X 0.946 | = Litres (l) | X 1.057 | = US quarts (US qt) |
| Imperial gallons (Imp gal) | X 4.546 | = Litres (l) | X 0.22 | = Imperial gallons (Irnp gal) |
| Imperial gallons (Imp gal) | X 1.201 | = US gallons (US gal) | X 0.833 | = Imperial gallons (Imp gal) |
| US gallons (US gal) | X 3.785 | = Litres (l) | X 0.264 | = US gallons (US gal) |

### Mass (weight)

| | | | | |
|---|---|---|---|---|
| Ounces (oz) | X 28.35 | = Grams (g) | X 0.035 | = Ounces (oz) |
| Pounds (lb) | X 0.454 | = Kilograms (kg) | X 2.205 | = Pounds (lb) |

### Force

| | | | | |
|---|---|---|---|---|
| Ounces-force (ozf; oz) | X 0.278 | = Newtons (N) | X 3.6 | = Ounces-force (ozf; oz) |
| Pounds-force (lbf; lb) | X 4.448 | = Newtons (N) | X 0.225 | = Pounds-force (lbf; lb) |
| Newtons (N) | X 0.1 | = Kilograms-force (kgf; kg) | X 9.81 | = Newtons (N) |

### Pressure

| | | | | |
|---|---|---|---|---|
| Pounds-force per square inch (psi; lbf/in$^2$; lb/in$^2$) | X 0.070 | = Kilograms-force per square centimetre (kgf/cm$^2$; kg/cm$^2$) | X 14.223 | = Pounds-force per square inch (psi; lbf/in$^2$; lb/in$^2$) |
| Pounds-force per square inch (psi; lbf/in$^2$; lb/in$^2$) | X 0.068 | = Atmospheres (atm) | X 14.696 | = Pounds-force per square inch (psi; lbf/in$^2$; lb/in$^2$) |
| Pounds-force per square inch (psi; lbf/in$^2$; lb/in$^2$) | X 0.069 | = Bars | X 14.5 | = Pounds-force per square inch (psi; lbf/in$^2$; lb/in$^2$) |
| Pounds-force per square inch (psi; lbf/in$^2$; lb/in$^2$) | X 6.895 | = Kilopascals (kPa) | X 0.145 | = Pounds-force per square inch (psi; lbf/in$^2$; lb/in$^2$) |
| Kilopascals (kPa) | X 0.01 | = Kilograms-force per square centimetre (kgf/cm$^2$; kg/cm$^2$) | X 98.1 | = Kilopascals (kPa) |

### Torque (moment of force)

| | | | | |
|---|---|---|---|---|
| Pounds-force inches (lbf in; lb in) | X 1.152 | = Kilograms-force centimetre (kgf cm; kg cm) | X 0.868 | = Pounds-force inches (lbf in; lb in) |
| Pounds-force inches (lbf in; lb in) | X 0.113 | = Newton metres (Nm) | X 8.85 | = Pounds-force inches (lbf in; lb in) |
| Pounds-force inches (lbf in; lb in) | X 0.083 | = Pounds-force feet (lbf ft; lb ft) | X 12 | = Pounds-force inches (lbf in; lb in) |
| Pounds-force feet (lbf ft; lb ft) | X 0.138 | = Kilograms-force metres (kgf m; kg m) | X 7.233 | = Pounds-force feet (lbf ft; lb ft) |
| Pounds-force feet (lbf ft; lb ft) | X 1.356 | = Newton metres (Nm) | X 0.738 | = Pounds-force feet (lbf ft; lb ft) |
| Newton metres (Nm) | X 0.102 | = Kilograms-force metres (kgf m; kg m) | X 9.804 | = Newton metres (Nm) |

### Power

| | | | | |
|---|---|---|---|---|
| Horsepower (hp) | X 745.7 | = Watts (W) | X 0.0013 | = Horsepower (hp) |

### Velocity (speed)

| | | | | |
|---|---|---|---|---|
| Miles per hour (miles/hr; mph) | X 1.609 | = Kilometres per hour (km/hr; kph) | X 0.621 | = Miles per hour (miles/hr; mph) |

### Fuel consumption*

| | | | | |
|---|---|---|---|---|
| Miles per gallon, Imperial (mpg) | X 0.354 | = Kilometres per litre (km/l) | X 2.825 | = Miles per gallon, Imperial (mpg) |
| Miles per gallon, US (mpg) | X 0.425 | = Kilometres per litre (km/l) | X 2.352 | = Miles per gallon, US (mpg) |

### Temperature

Degrees Fahrenheit = (°C x 1.8) + 32

Degrees Celsius (Degrees Centigrade; °C) = (°F - 32) x 0.56

*It is common practice to convert from miles per gallon (mpg) to litres/100 kilometres (l/100km), where mpg (Imperial) x l/100 km = 282 and mpg (US) x l/100 km = 235

# Index

**Printed by
Haynes Publishing Group
Sparkford Yeovil Somerset
England**